The Sovereignty of Good

'The theme is the inadequacy of the account of human nature and value provided by contemporary, academic analytic philosophy. Murdoch's attack is the fruit of a thorough professional involvement with the school of thought to which she is opposed.'

Anthony Quinton, The Sunday Telegraph

'All three essays which make up this book are superb. ... She has carefully pondered all that logical analysis, existentialism, Marxism, Freudianism can say, has learned from them, and yet is able to present an old-fashioned view with complete modernity.'

Martin Jarrett-Kerr, The Guardian

'The project of founding morality not on changing human needs or wishes but on an immutable and absolute idea of goodness has been central to her thought.'

Mary Warnock, Women Philosophers

Routledge Classics contains the very best of Routledge publishing over the past century or so, books that have, by popular consent, become established as classics in their field. Drawing on a fantastic heritage of innovative writing published by Routledge and its associated imprints, this series makes available in attractive, affordable form some of the most important works of modern times.

For a complete list of titles visit
www.routledgeclassics.com

Iris
Murdoch

The Sovereignty of Good

London and New York

First published 1970
by Routledge & Kegan Paul

First published in Routledge Classics 2001
by Routledge
2 Park Square, Milton Park, Abingdon, Oxon, OX14 4RN
711 Third Avenue, New York, NY 10017 (8th Floor)
Routledge is an imprint of the Taylor & Francis Group, an informa business

© 1971 Iris Murdoch

Typeset in Joanna by RefineCatch Limited, Bungay, Suffolk

British Library Cataloguing in Publication Data
A catalogue record for this book is available from the British Library

ISBN 13: 978–0–415–25552–3 (hbk)
ISBN 13: 978–0–415–25399–4 (pbk)

CONTENTS

PREFACE

These three papers have been in print before. I should like to thank the editor for permission to reprint 'The Idea of Perfection' from the *Yale Review* 1964, the Syndics of the Cambridge University Press for permission to reprint 'The Sovereignty of Good Over Other Concepts', which was the Leslie Stephen Lecture for 1967, and Professor Marjorie Grene and the Study Group on Foundations of Cultural Unity and Routledge and Kegan Paul for permission to reprint 'On "God" and "Good"', published in *The Anatomy of Knowledge*, 1969. 'The Idea of Perfection' is based upon the Ballard Mathews lecture which I delivered in the University College of North Wales in 1962.

Iris Murdoch

1

THE IDEA OF PERFECTION

It is sometimes said, either irritably or with a certain satisfaction, that philosophy makes no progress. It is certainly true, and I think this is an abiding and not a regrettable characteristic of the discipline, that philosophy has in a sense to keep trying to return to the beginning: a thing which it is not at all easy to do. There is a two-way movement in philosophy, a movement towards the building of elaborate theories, and a move back again towards the consideration of simple and obvious facts. McTaggart says that time is unreal, Moore replies that he has just had his breakfast. Both these aspects of philosophy are necessary to it.

I wish in this discussion to attempt a movement of return, a retracing of our steps to see how a certain position was reached. The position in question, in current moral philosophy, is one which seems to me unsatisfactory in two related ways, in that it ignores certain facts and at the same time imposes a single theory which admits of no communication with or escape into rival theories. If it is true that philosophy has almost always done this, it is also true that philosophers have never put up with it for very long. Instances of the facts, as I shall boldly call them, which interest me and which seem to have been forgotten or 'theorized away' are the fact that an unexamined life can be virtuous and the fact that love is a central concept in morals. Contemporary philosophers frequently connect consciousness with virtue, and although they constantly talk of freedom they rarely talk of love. But there must be some relation between these latter concepts, and it must be possible to do justice to both Socrates and the virtuous peasant. In such 'musts' as these lie the deepest springs and motives of philosophy. Yet if in an attempt to enlarge our field of vision we turn for a moment to philosophical theories outside our own tradition we find it very difficult to establish any illuminating connection.

Professor Hampshire says, in the penultimate chapter of *Thought and Action*, that 'it is the constructive task of a philosophy of mind to provide a set of terms in which ultimate judgements of value can be very clearly stated.' In this understanding of it, philosophy of mind is the background to moral philosophy; and in so far as modern ethics tends to constitute a sort of Newspeak which makes certain values non-expressible, the reasons for this are to be sought in current philosophy of mind and in the fascinating power of a certain picture of the soul. One suspects that philosophy of mind has not in fact been performing the task, which Professor Hampshire recommends, of sorting and classifying fundamental moral issues; it has rather been imposing upon us a particular value judgment in the guise of a theory of human nature. Whether philosophy can ever do anything else is a question we shall have to consider. But in so far as modern philosophers profess to be analytic and neutral any failure to be so deserves comment. And an attempt to produce, if not a comprehensive analysis, at least a rival soul-picture which covers a greater or a different territory should make new places for philosophical reflection. We would like to know what, as moral agents, we have got to do because of logic, what we have got to do because of human nature, and what we can choose to do. Such a programme is easy to state and perhaps impossible to carry out. But even to discover what, under these headings, we *can* achieve certainly demands a much more complex and subtle conceptual system than any which we can find readily available.

Before going on to consider the problems in philosophy of mind which underlie the inarticulate moments of modern ethics I should like to say a word about G. E. Moore. Moore is as it were the frame of the picture. A great deal has happened since he wrote, and when we read him again it is startling to see how many of his beliefs are philosophically unstatable now. Moore believed that good was a supersensible reality, that it was a mysterious quality, unrepresentable and indefinable, that it was an object of knowledge and (implicitly) that to be able to see it was in some sense to have it. He thought of the good upon the analogy of the beautiful; and he was, in spite of himself, a 'naturalist' in that he took goodness to be a real constituent of the world. We know how severely and in what respects Moore was corrected by his successors. Moore was quite right (it was said) to separate the question 'What does "good" mean?' from the question 'What things are good?' though he was wrong to answer the second question as well as the first. He was right to say that good was indefinable, but wrong to say that it was the name of a quality. Good is indefinable because judgments of value depend upon the will and choice of the individual. Moore was wrong (his critics continue) to use the quasi-aesthetic imagery of vision in conceiving the good. Such a view, conceiving the good on the analogy of the beautiful, would seem to make possible a contemplative attitude on the part of the moral agent, whereas the point about this person is that he is essentially and inescapably an *agent*. The image whereby to understand morality, it is argued, is not the image of vision but the image of movement. Goodness and beauty are not analogous but sharply contrasting ideas. Good must be thought of, not as part of the world, but as a movable label affixed to the world; for only so can the agent be pictured as responsible and free. And indeed this truth Moore himself half apprehended when he separated the denotation from the connotation of 'good'. The concept 'good' is not the name of an esoteric object, it is the tool of every rational man. Goodness is not an object of insight or knowledge, it is a function of the will. Thus runs the correction of Moore; and let me say in anticipation that on almost every point I agree with Moore and not with his critics.

The idea that 'good' is a function of the will stunned philosophy with its attractiveness, since it solved so many problems at one blow: metaphysical entities were removed, and moral judgments were seen to be, not weird statements, but something much more comprehensible, such as persuasions or commands or rules. The idea has its own obviousness: but it does not depend for its plausibility solely upon its usefulness or upon an appeal to our ordinary knowledge of the moral life. It coheres with a whole moral psychology, much of which has been elaborated more recently. I want now to examine certain aspects of this psychology and to trace it to what I think is its origin and basis in a certain argument of Wittgenstein. First I shall sketch 'the man' which this psychology presents us with, then I shall comment on this man's most important features, and then I shall proceed to consider the radical arguments for such an image.

I shall use for my picture of 'the man' of modern moral philosophy two works of Professor Hampshire, his book *Thought and Action* and his lecture *Disposition and Memory*. Hampshire's view is, I think, without commanding universal agreement, fairly central and typical, and it has the great merit that it states and elaborates what in many modern moral philosophers is simply taken for granted. Hampshire suggests that we should abandon the image (dear to the British empiricists) of man as a detached observer, and should rather picture him as an object moving among other objects in a continual flow of intention into action.

Touch and movement, not vision, should supply our metaphors: 'Touching, handling and the manipulation of things are misrepresented if we follow the analogy of vision.' Actions are, roughly, instances of moving things about in the public world. Nothing counts as an act unless it is a 'bringing about of a recognizable change in the world'. What sorts of things can be such recognizable changes? Here we must distinguish between 'the things and persons that constitute the external world and the sensations and impressions that I or anyone else may from moment to moment enjoy'. What is 'real' is potentially open to different observers. The inner or mental world is inevitably parasitic upon the outer world, it has 'a parasitic and shadowy nature'. The definiteness of any thought process depends upon 'the possibility of [its] being recognized, scrutinized and identified by observers from different points of view; this possibility is essential to any definite reality'. 'The play of the mind, free of any expression in audible speech or visible action is a reality, as the play of shadows is a reality. But any description of it is derived from the description of its natural expression in speech and action.' 'The assent that takes place within the mind and in no process of communication when no question has been actually asked and answered is a shadowy assent and a shadowy act.' 'Thought cannot be thought, as opposed to day-dreaming or musing, unless it is directed towards a conclusion, whether in action or in judgement.' Further: thought and belief are separate from will and action. 'We do try, in ordinary speech and thought, to keep the distinction between thought and action as definite as possible.' Thought as such is not action but an introduction to action. 'That which I do is that for which I am responsible and which is peculiarly an expression of myself. It is essential to thought that it takes its own forms and follows its own paths without my intervention, that is, without the intervention of my will. I identify myself with my will. Thought, when it is most pure, is self-directing. . . . Thought begins on its own path, governed by its universal rules, when the preliminary work of the will is done. No process of thought could be punctuated by acts of will, voluntary switchings of attention, and retain its status as a continuous process of thought.' These are very important assumptions. It will follow from this that a 'belief' is not something subject to the will. 'It seems that I cannot present my own belief in something as an achievement, because, by so presenting it, I would disqualify it as belief.' These quotations are from *Thought and Action*, the later part of Chapter Two.

In the Ernest Jones lecture, *Disposition and Memory*, Hampshire does two things: he puts the arguments of *Thought and Action* more polemically in a nutshell, and he introduces, under the protection of Freud, an idea of 'personal verification' which I shall discuss at length below. From *Disposition and Memory*: 'Intention is the one concept that ought to be preserved free from any taint of the less than conscious.' And 'it is characteristic of mental, as opposed to physical, concepts that the conditions of their application can only be understood if they are analysed genetically'. These are succinct statements of what has already been argued in *Thought and Action*. Hampshire now gives us in addition a picture of 'the ideally rational man'. This person would be 'aware of all his memories as memories. . . . His wishes would be attached to definite possibilities in a definite future. . . . He would . . . distinguish his present situation from unconscious memories of the past . . . and would find his motives for action in satisfying his instinctual needs within the objectively observed features of the situation.' This ideal man does not exist because the palimpsest of 'dispositions' is too hard to penetrate: and this is just as well because ideal rationality would leave us 'without art, without dream or imagination, without likes or dislikes unconnected with instinctual needs'. In theory, though not in practice, 'an interminable analysis' could lay bare the dispositional machinery and make possible a perfect prediction of conduct;

but Hampshire emphasizes (and this is the main point of the lecture) that such ideal knowledge would not take the form of a scientific law but would have its basis and its verification in the history of the individual. I shall argue later that the very persuasive image with which Hampshire has presented us contains incompatible elements. Roughly, there is a conflict between the 'logical' view of the mind and the 'historical' view of the mind, a conflict which exists partly because logic is still tied to an old-fashioned conception of science. But this is to anticipate.

I shall find it useful later to define my own view in fairly exact section-by-section contrast with Hampshire's; and as his view is rich in detail, extensive quotation has been necessary. As I have suggested, Hampshire's man is to be found more or less explicitly lurking behind much that is written nowadays on the subject of moral philosophy and indeed also of politics. Hampshire has thoroughly explored a background which many writers have taken for granted: and for this one is grateful. This 'man', one may add, is familiar to us for another reason: he is the hero of almost every contemporary novel. Let us look at his characteristics, noting them as yet without discussion. Hampshire emphasizes clarity of intention. He says 'all problems meet in intention', and he utters in relation to intention the only explicit 'ought' in his psychology. We ought to know what we are doing. We should aim at total knowledge of our situation and a clear conceptualization of all our possibilities. Thought and intention must be directed towards definite overt issues or else they are merely day-dream. 'Reality' is potentially open to different observers. What is 'inward', what lies in between overt actions, is either impersonal thought, or 'shadows' of acts, or else substanceless dream. Mental life is, and logically must be, a shadow of life in public. Our personal being is the movement of our overtly choosing will. Immense care is taken to picture the will as isolated. It is isolated from belief, from reason, from feeling, and is yet the essential centre of the self. 'I identify myself with my will.' It is separated from belief so that the authority of reason, which manufactures belief; may be entire and so that responsibility for action may be entire as well. My responsibility is a function of my knowledge (which tries to be wholly impersonal) and my will (which is wholly personal). Morality is a matter of thinking clearly and then proceeding to outward dealings with other men.

On this view one might say that morality is assimilated to a visit to a shop. I enter the shop in a condition of totally responsible freedom, I objectively estimate the features of the goods, and I choose. The greater my objectivity and discrimination the larger the number of products from which I can select. (A Marxist critique of this conception of bourgeois capitalist morals would be apt enough. Should we want many goods in the shop or just 'the right goods'?) Both as act and reason, shopping is public. Will does not bear upon reason, so the 'inner life' is not to be thought of as a moral sphere. Reason deals in neutral descriptions and aims at being the frequently mentioned ideal observer. Value terminology will be the prerogative of the will; but since will is pure choice, pure movement, and not thought or vision, will really requires only action words such as 'good' or 'right'. It is not characteristic of the man we are describing, as he appears either in textbooks or in fiction, to possess an elaborate normative vocabulary. Modern ethics analyses 'good', the empty action word which is the correlate of the isolated will, and tends to ignore other value terms. Our hero aims at being a 'realist' and regards sincerity as the fundamental and perhaps the only virtue.

The very powerful image with which we are here presented is behaviourist, existentialist, and utilitarian in a sense which unites these three conceptions. It is behaviourist in its connection of the meaning and being of action with the publicly observable, it is existentialist in its elimination of the substantial self and its emphasis on the solitary omnipotent will, and it is utilitarian in its assumption that morality is and can only be concerned with public acts.) It is also incidentally what may be called a democratic view, in that it suggests that morality is not an esoteric achievement but a natural function of any normal man. This position represents, to put it in another way, a happy and fruitful marriage of Kantian liberalism with Wittgensteinian logic solemnized by Freud. But this also is to anticipate; what confronts us here is in fact complex and difficult to analyse. Let me now try to sort out and classify the different questions which need to be answered.

I find the image of man which I have sketched above both alien and implausible. That is, more precisely: I have simple empirical objections (I do not think people are necessarily or essentially 'like that'), I have philosophical objections (I do not find the arguments convincing), and I have moral objections (I do not think people *ought* to picture themselves in this way). It is a delicate and tricky matter to keep these kinds of objections separate in one's mind. Later on I shall try to present my own rival picture. But now first of all I want to examine in more detail the theory of the 'inner life' with which we have been presented. One's initial reaction to this theory is likely to be a strong instinctive one: either one will be content with the emphasis on the reality of the outer, the absence of the inner, or one will feel (as I do) it cannot be so, something vital is missing. And if one thinks that somehow or other 'the inner' is important one will be the more zealous in criticizing the arguments concerning its status. Such criticisms may have far-reaching results, since upon the question of 'what goes on inwardly' in between moments of overt 'movement' depends our view of the status of choice, the meaning of freedom, and the whole problem of the relation of will to reason and intellect to desire. I shall now consider what I think is the most radical argument, the keystone, of this existentialist-behaviourist type of moral psychology: the argument to the effect that mental concepts must be analysed genetically and so the inner must be thought of as parasitic upon the outer.

This argument is best understood as a special case of a yet more general and by now very familiar argument about the status of what is 'private'. Our tradition of philosophy, since Descartes until very recently, has been obsessed by an entity which has had various names: the *cogitatio*, the sense-impression, the sense-datum. This entity, private to each person, was thought of as an *appearance* about which the owner had infallible and certain *knowledge*. It was taken by Descartes as the starting point of a famous argument, and was pictured by the British empiricists as an instrument of thought. The conception of the *cogitatio* or sense-datum, oddly attractive and readily grasped, suggests among other things that what is inward may be private in one of two senses, one a contingent sense and one a logical sense. I can tell you, or refrain from telling you, a secret; but I cannot (logically) show you my sense-data.

After a long and varied history this conception has now been largely abandoned by philosophers. The general argument for abandoning it has two prongs. Briefly, the argument against the *cogitatio* is that (a) such an entity cannot form part of the structure of a public concept, (b) such an entity cannot be introspectively discovered. That is, (a) it's no use, (b) it isn't there. The latter point may be further subdivided into an empirical and a logical contention. The empirical contention is that there are very few and pretty hazy introspectabilia, and the logical contention is that there are in any case difficulties about their identification. Of the two moments in the general argument (a) has received more attention than (b), since as (a) has been regarded as knock-down (b) has been treated as subsidiary. If something is no use it does not matter much whether it's there or not. I shall argue shortly that because something is no use it has been too hastily assumed that something else is not there. But let us first look at the argument in more detail.

I said that the argument about mental concepts was a special case of the general argument. The general argument is at its most felicitous when applied to some simple non-mental concept such as 'red'. 'Red' cannot be the name of something private. The structure of the concept is its public structure, which is established by coinciding procedures in public situations. How much success we can have in establishing any given public structure will be an empirical question. The alleged inner thing can neither be known (Descartes) nor used (the British empiricists). Hume was wrong to worry about the missing shade of blue, not because a man could or couldn't picture it, or that we could or couldn't be persuaded that he had, but because the inner picture is necessarily irrelevant and the possession of the concept is a public skill. What matters is whether I stop at the traffic lights, and not my colour imagery or absence of it. I identify what my senses show me by means of the public schemata which I have learned, and in no other way can this be *known* by me, since knowledge involves the rigidity supplied by a public test. Wittgenstein in the *Untersuchungen* sums the situation up as follows: 'If we construe the grammar of the expression of sensation on the model of "object and name", the object drops out of consideration as irrelevant.'

This argument, which bears down relentlessly upon the case of 'red', might seem to be even more relentless in the case of the very much more shadowy inner entities which might be supposed to be the 'objects' of which mental concepts are 'names'. After all, one might say to oneself in a quasi-nonsensical way, my sensation of red does, when I am doing philosophy, look like something which I have privately 'got'; and if I am not allowed to 'keep' even this clear little thing as my own private datum, why should I expect to 'keep' the hopelessly hazy inner phenomena connected with concepts such as 'decision' and 'desire'? Surely I should in the latter cases be even happier to rely upon the 'outer' face of the concept, since the inner one is so vague. Let me clarify this so as to make plain the force of the genetic argument in the case of mental concepts.

Wittgenstein of course discusses in this context mental as well as physical concepts. But his discussion is marked by a peculiar reticence. He does not make any moral or psychological generalizations. He limits himself to observing that a mental concept verb used in the first person is not a report about something private, since in the absence of any checking procedure it makes no sense to speak of oneself being either right or mistaken. Wittgenstein is not claiming that inner data are 'incommunicable', nor that anything special about human personality follows from their 'absence', he is merely saying that no sense can be attached to the idea of an 'inner object'. There are no 'private ostensive definitions'. Whether Wittgenstein is right to say that we can attach no sense to the idea of being mistaken about how things *seem*, and whether any legitimate conclusions about human nature can be drawn from his position I shall consider later. I want now to go on to look at the conclusions which *have* (not by him) been drawn, and at the developed form of the argument as we find it, with variations, in Hampshire, Hare, Ayer, Ryle and others.

As I have said, the argument seems to bear even more strongly in proportion as the alleged inner datum becomes more obviously shadowy and even tends to be irresponsibly absent. In such cases purely empirical considerations (the empirical subdivision of (b) above) are especially strong. I say, 'Well, I must decide. All right. I'll go.' Perhaps nothing introspectible occurs at all? And even if it does *that* is not the decision. Here we see what is meant by speaking of a genetical analysis. How do I *learn* the concept of decision? By watching someone who says 'I have decided' and who then acts. How else could I learn it? And with that I learn the essence of the matter. I do not 'move on' from a behaviouristic concept to a mental one. (Since ordinary language, which 'misleadingly' connects the mental with the inner, straight-forwardly connects the physical with the outer, a genetic analysis of physical concepts would not be especially revealing.) A decision does not turn out to be, when more carefully considered, an introspectible movement. The concept has no further inner structure; it is its outer structure. Take an even clearer example. How do I distinguish anger from jealousy? Certainly not by discriminating between two kinds of private mental data. Consider how I *learned* 'anger' and 'jealousy'. What identifies the emotion is the presence not of a particular private object, but of some typical outward behaviour pattern. This will also imply, be it noted, that we can be mistaken in the names which we give to our own mental states.

This is the point at which people may begin to protest and cry out and say that something has been taken from them. Surely there is such a thing as deciding and not acting? Surely there are *private* decisions? Surely there are lots and lots of objects, more or less easily identified, in orbit as it were in inner space? It is not, as the argument would seem to imply, silent and dark within. Philosophers will reply coolly to these protests. Of course a sense can be attached to: he decided to but did not. That is, he said he would go, and we had reasons to believe that he would, but a brick fell on his head. Or, the notion of his going cohered with many other things he was doing and saying, and yet he did not go. But all this is just as overt, just as little private, as the actual carrying out of the decision. And it must be admitted to be, when one reflects, difficult to attach sense by any other method to the idea of an unfulfilled decision, in our own case just as much as in the case of someone else. Are there 'private' decisions? I said some words to myself. But did I really decide? To answer that question I examine the *context* of my announcement rather than its private core.

However, it will be said, surely there *are* introspectible objects which we can identify? We *do* have images, talk to ourselves, etc. Does the genetic argument imply that these are nothing? Well, it might be answered, let us look at them. One might roughly divide these data in order of shadowiness into visual images, verbal thoughts, other images, other thoughts and feelings which while not exactly verbal or visual seem nevertheless to be 'entities'. It will be true of all these that I cannot show them to other people. Of course I can to a limited extent describe them, I can describe my imagery or mention words which 'say' in my head. I can also give metaphorical descriptions of my states of mind. (Ryle discusses these 'chronicles' and 'histories' of thought in *Aristotelian Society Supplementary Volume* 1952). But what does this amount to? These data, vaguer and more infrequent than one might unreflectively suppose, cannot claim to be 'the thing itself' of which my uttered thoughts are the report. Note that I offer my descriptions in ordinary public words whose meaning is subject to ordinary public rules. Inner words 'mean' in the same way as outer words; and I can only 'know' my imagery because I know the public things which it is 'of'. Public concepts are in this obvious sense sovereign over private objects; I can only 'identify' the inner, even for my own bene-fit, via my knowledge of the outer. But in any case there is no check upon the accuracy of such descriptions, and as Wittgen-stein says, 'What is this ceremony for?' Who, except possibly empirical psychologists, is interested in alleged reports of what is *purely* inward? And psychologists themselves now have grave doubts about the value of such 'evidence' from introspection. Whether I am *really* thinking about so-and-so or deciding such-and-such or feeling angry or jealous or pleased will be prop-erly determined, and can only be determined, by the overt context, however sketchy and embryonic. That I decided to do X will be true if I said sincerely that I was going to and did it, even if nothing introspectible occurred at all. And equally something introspectible might occur, but if the outward context is entirely lacking the something cannot be called a decision. As Wittgenstein puts it, 'a wheel that can be turned though nothing else moves with it is not part of the mechanism'.

These radical arguments are, it seems to me, perfectly sound over a certain range. They really do clearly and definitively solve certain problems which have beset British empiricism. By destroying the misleading image of the infallible inner eye they make possible a much improved solution of, for instance, problems about perception and about universals. A great deal that was, in Hume and Berkeley, repugnant to common sense can now be cleared away. But, as I have said, while Wittgenstein remains sphinx-like in the background, others have hastened to draw further and more dubious moral and psychological conclusions. Wittgenstein has created a void into which neo-Kantianism, existentialism, utilitarianism have made haste to enter. And notice how plausibly the arguments, their prestige enhanced from undoubted success in other fields, seem to support, indeed to impose, the image of personality which I have sketched above. As the 'inner life' is hazy, largely absent, and any way 'not part of the mechanism', it turns out to be *logically* impossible to take up an idle contemplative attitude to the good. Morality must be action since mental concepts can only be analysed genetically. Metaphors of movement and not vision seem obviously appropriate. Morality, with the full support of logic, abhors the private. Salvation by works is a conceptual necessity. *What* I am doing or being is not something private and personal, but is imposed upon me in the sense of being identifiable only via public concepts and objective observers. Self-knowledge is something which shows overtly. Reasons are public reasons, rules are public rules. Reason and rule represent a sort of impersonal tyranny in relation to which however the personal will represents perfect freedom. The machinery is relentless, but until the moment of choice the agent is outside the machinery. Morality resides at the point of action. What I am 'objectively' is not under my control; logic and observers decide that. What I am 'subjectively' is a foot-loose, solitary, substanceless will. Personality dwindles to a point of pure will.

Now it is not at all easy to mount an attack upon this heavily fortified position; and, as I say, temperament will play its part in determining whether or not we *want* to attack or whether we are content. I am not content. Let me start cautiously to suggest an alternative view, taking however for a rubric the warning words of Wittgenstein: 'Being unable—when we surrender ourselves to philosophical thought—to help saying such-and-such; being irresistibly inclined to say it—does not mean being forced into an *assumption*, or having an immediate perception or knowledge of a state of affairs.'

For purposes of the rest of this discussion it will be useful to have an example before us: some object which we can all more or less see, and to which we can from time to time refer. All sorts of different things would do for this example, and I was at first tempted to take a case of *ritual* for instance a religious ritual wherein the inner consent appears to be the real act. Ritual: an outer framework which both occasions and identifies an inner event. It can be argued that I make a promise by uttering the words 'I promise': a performative utterance. But do I, in a religious context, repent by sincerely uttering the words 'I repent', am I 'heartily sorry' simply by saying in an appropriate situation that I am heartily sorry? Is this so even if I then amend my life? This is not so clear and is indeed a difficult and interesting question. I decided however not to take a religious example, which might be felt to raise special difficulties, but to take something more ordinary and everyday. So here is the example.

A mother, whom I shall call M, feels hostility to her daughter-in-law, whom I shall call D. M finds D quite a good-hearted girl, but while not exactly common yet certainly unpolished and lacking in dignity and refinement. D is inclined to be pert and familiar, insufficiently ceremonious, brusque, sometimes positively rude, always tiresomely juvenile. M does not like D's accent or the way D dresses. M feels that her son has married beneath him. Let us assume for purposes of the example that the mother, who is a very 'correct' person, behaves beautifully to the girl throughout, not allowing her real opinion to appear in any way. We might underline this aspect of the example by supposing that the young couple have emigrated or that D is now dead: the point being to ensure that whatever is in question as *happening* happens entirely in M's mind.

Thus much for M's first thoughts about D. Time passes, and it could be that M settles down with a hardened sense of grievance and a fixed picture of D, imprisoned (if I may use a question-begging word) by the cliché: my poor son has married a silly vulgar girl. However, the M of the example is an intelligent and well-intentioned person, capable of self-criticism, capable of giving careful and just *attention* to an object which confronts her. M tells herself: 'I am old-fashioned and conventional. I may be prejudiced and narrow-minded. I may be snobbish. I am certainly jealous. Let me look again.' Here I assume that M observes D or at least reflects deliberately about D, until gradually her vision of D alters. If we take D to be now absent or dead this can make it clear that the change is not in D's behaviour but in M's mind. D is discovered to be not vulgar but refreshingly simple, not undignified but spontaneous, not noisy but gay, not tiresomely juvenile but delightfully youthful, and so on. And as I say, *ex hypothesi*, M's outward behaviour, beautiful from the start, in no way alters.

I used above words such as 'just' and 'intelligent' which implied a favourable value judgment on M's activity: and I want in fact to imagine a case where one would feel approval of M's change of view. But of course in real life, and this is of interest, it might be very hard to decide whether what M was doing was proper or not, and opinions might differ. M might be moved by various motives: a sense of justice, attempted love for D, love for her son, or simply reluctance to think of him as unfortunate or mistaken. Some people might say 'she deludes herself' while others would say she was moved by love or justice. I am picturing a case where I would find the latter description appropriate.

What *happens* in this example could of course be described in other ways. I have chosen to describe it simply in terms of the substitution of one set of normative epithets for another. It could also be described, for instance, in terms of M's visual imagery, or in simple or complex metaphors. But let us consider now what exactly 'it' is which is being described. It may be argued that there is nothing here which presents any special difficulty. For purposes of moral judgment we may define 'actions' in various ways. One way in this case would be to say that M decided to behave well to D and did so; and M's private thoughts will be unimportant and morally irrelevant. If however it is desired to include in the list of M's moral acts more than her overt behaviour shows, one will have to ask of the extra material: in what sense 'moral' and in what sense 'acts'? Of course if M's reflections were the prologue to *different* outer acts, then the reflections might be allowed to 'belong' to the acts as their 'shadows' and gain from them their identity and their importance: though the difficulty of discerning the inward part and connecting it with the outer as a condition of the latter could still be considerable. But what are we to say in the present case?

Hampshire tells us: 'Thought cannot be thought as opposed to day-dreaming or musing, unless it is directed towards a conclusion, whether in action or in judgement. . . . The idea of thought as an interior monologue . . . will become altogether empty if the thought does not even purport to be directed towards its issue in the external world. . . . Under these conditions thought and belief would not differ from the charmed and habitual rehearsal of phrases or the drifting of ideas through the mind.' Let us exclude from this discussion something which might at this point try to enter it, which is the eye of God. If M's mental events are not to depend for being and importance upon this metaphysical witness, do we want to, and if so how can we, rescue them from the fate of being mere nothings, at best describable as day-dreams?

It would be possible of course to give a *hypothetical* status to M's inner life, as follows. 'M's vision of D has altered *means* that if M were to speak her mind about D now she would say different things from the things she would have said three years ago.' This analysis avoids some difficulties but, like phenomenalism, encounters others. The truth of the hypothetical proposition could be consistent with nothing in the interim having occurred in M's mind at all. And of course a change of mind often does take the form of the simple announcement of a new view without any introspectible material having intervened. But here *ex hypothesi* there is at least something introspectible which has occurred, however hazy this may be, and it is the status of this which is in question. At any rate the idea which we are trying to make sense of is that M has in the interim been *active*, she has been *doing* something, something which we approve of, something which is somehow worth doing in itself. M has been morally active in the interim: this is what we want to say and to be philosophically permitted to say.

At this point the defender of what I have called the existentialist-behaviourist view may argue as follows. All right. Either M has no introspectible material, in which case since M's conduct is constant it is hard to see what could be meant by saying that she had changed her mind, other than saying that a hypothetical proposition is true which no one could know to be true; or else M has introspectible material and let us see what this might be like. M may imagine saying things to D, may verbally describe D in her mind, may brood on visual images of D. But what do these goings-on mean? What is to count here as serious judgment as opposed to 'the charmed and habitual rehearsal of phrases?' M's introspectabilia are likely on examination to prove hazy and hard to describe; and even if (at best) we imagine M as making clear verbal statements to herself, the identity and meaning of these statements is a function of the public world. She can only be thought of as 'speaking' seriously, and not parrot-like, if the outer context logically permits.

The point can also be made, it may be said in parenthesis, that the identity of inward thoughts is established via the public meaning of the symbolism used in thinking. (See, e.g., Ayer, Thinking and Meaning.) This should refute claims to 'ineffable experience', etc. Philosophers have more recently chosen to emphasize the 'shadow' view, that is to consider the particular sense of the thought via context rather than the general sense of the thought via symbols. But I think the points are worth separating. They represent two complementary pictures of the 'self' or 'will' as outside the network of logical rules, free to decide where to risk its tyranny, but thereafter caught in an impersonal complex. I can decide what to say but not what the words mean which I have said. I can decide what to do but I am not master of the significance of my act.

Someone who says privately or overtly 'I have decided' but who never acts, however favourable the circumstances (the existentialist-behaviourist argument continues), has not decided. Private decisions which precede public actions may be thought of as the 'shadow' of the act, gaining their title from being part of a complex properly called 'decision': though even here the term 'decision' if applied to the inner part only would be a courtesy title since there is no check upon the nature or existence of the inner part and its connection with the outer. Still, that is the situation in which we innocuously and popularly speak of 'private decisions' or 'inner acts', i.e., where some kind of outer structure is present and we may if we like picture, perhaps we naturally picture, an inner piece too. In M's case, however, since there is no outward alteration of structure to correspond to an alleged inner change, no sequence of outer events of which the inner can claim to be shadows, it is dubious whether any sense can be given here to the idea of 'activity'. The attempted categorical sense of M's inner progress has to fall back on the hypothetical sense mentioned above. And the hypothetical proposition cannot be known to be true, even by M, and could be true without anything happening in M's mind at all. So the idea of M as *inwardly* active turns out to be an empty one. There is only outward activity, ergo only outward moral activity, and what we call inward activity is merely the shadow of this cast back into the mind. And, it may be bracingly added, why worry? As Kant said, what we are commanded to do is to love our neighbour in a practical and not a pathological sense.

This is one of those exasperating moments in philosophy when one seems to be being relentlessly prevented from saying something which one is irresistibly impelled to say. And of course, as Wittgenstein pointed out, the fact that one is irresistibly impelled to say it need not mean that anything *else* is the case. Let us tread carefully here. In reacting against the above analysis there is certainly one thing which I do *not* wish to maintain, and that is that we have infallible or superior knowledge of our mental states. We can be mistaken about what we think and feel: that is not in dispute, and indeed it is a strength of the behaviourist analysis that it so neatly accommodates this fact. What is at stake is something different, something about *activity* in a sense which does not mean privileged activity.

Let me try in a rough ordinary way and as yet without justification to say what I take to be, in spite of the analysis, the case about M: a view which is not congruent with the analysis and which if true shows that the analysis cannot be correct. The analysis pictures M as defined 'from the outside in': M's individuality lies in her will, understood as her 'movements'. The analysis makes no sense of M as continually active, as making progress, or of her inner acts as belonging to her or forming part of a continuous fabric of being: it is precisely critical of metaphors such as 'fabric of being'. Yet can we do without such metaphors here? Further, is not the metaphor of vision almost irresistibly suggested to anyone who, without philosophical prejudice, wishes to describe the situation? Is it not the natural metaphor? M *looks* at D, she attends to D, she focuses her attention. M is engaged in an internal struggle. She may for instance be tempted to enjoy caricatures of D in her imagination. (There is curiously little place in the other picture for the idea of *struggle*.) And M's activity here, so far from being something very odd and hazy, is something which, in a way, we find exceedingly familiar. Innumerable novels contain accounts of what such struggles are like. Anybody could describe one without being at a loss for words. This activity, as I said, could be described in a variety of ways, but one very natural way is by the use of specialized normative words, what one might call the secondary moral words in contrast to the primary and general ones such as 'good'. M stops seeing D as 'bumptious' and sees her as 'gay', etc. I shall comment later upon the importance of these secondary words. Further again, one feels impelled to say something like: M's activity is peculiarly *her own*. Its details are the details of this personality; and partly for this reason it may well be an activity which can only be performed privately. M could not *do* this thing in conversation with another person. Hampshire says that 'anything which is to count as a definite reality must be open to several observers'. But can this quasi-scientific notion of individuation through unspecified observers really be applied to a case like this? Here there is an activity but no observers; and if one were to introduce the idea of potential observers the question of their *competence* would still arise. M's activity is hard to characterize not because it is hazy but *precisely because it is moral*. And with this, as I shall shortly try to explain, we are coming near to the centre of the difficulty.

What M is *ex hypothesi* attempting to do is not just to see D accurately but to see her justly or lovingly. Notice the rather different image of freedom which this at once suggests. Freedom is not the sudden jumping of the isolated will in and out of an impersonal logical complex, it is a function of the progressive attempt to see a particular object clearly. M's activity is essentially something progressive, something infinitely perfectible. So far from claiming for it a sort of infallibility, this new picture has built in the notion of a necessary fallibility. M is engaged in an endless task. As soon as we begin to use words such as 'love' and 'justice' in characterizing M, we introduce into our whole conceptual picture of her situation the idea of progress, that is the idea of perfection: and it is just the presence of this idea which demands an analysis of mental concepts which is different from the genetic one.

I am now inclined to think that it is pointless, when faced with the existentialist-behaviourist picture of the mind, to go on endlessly fretting about the identification of particular inner events, and attempting to defend an account of M as 'active' by producing, as it were, a series of indubitably objective little things. 'Not a report' need not entail 'not an activity'. But to elaborate this what is needed is some sort of change of key, some moving of the attack to a different front. Let us consider for a moment the apparently so plausible idea of identity as dependent upon observers and rules, an idea which leads on directly to the genetic analysis of mental concepts. This is really red if several people agree about the description, indeed this is what being really red means. He really decided, roughly, if people agree that he kept the rules of the concept 'decide'. To decide means to keep these rules and the agent is not the only judge. Actions are 'moving things about in the public world', and what these movements *are* objective observers are actually and potentially at hand to decide.

Wittgenstein, as I have said, does not apply this idea to moral concepts, nor discuss its relation to mental concepts in so far as these form part of the sphere of morality. (That mental concepts enter the sphere of morality is, for my argument, precisely the central point.) But no limit is placed upon the idea either; and I should like to place a limit. What has enabled this idea of identification to go too far is partly, I think, an uncriticized conception of science which has taken on where Hume left off.

Hume pictured a manifold of atoms, hard little indubitable sense-data or appearances, whose 'subsequent' arrangement provided the so-called material world. The Copernican Revolution of modern philosophy ('You can't have "knowledge" of "appearances"') removes the notion of certainty from the inside to the outside: public rules now determine what is certain. It may still be disputed whether one cannot sometimes give a sense to 'being mistaken about an appearance'. There is certainly an area for discussion here, but this discussion has never become a very radical one. It has remained within the general terms of the revolution; and although it would be impossible to dispute the importance of that revolution it has nevertheless been so far in effect a continuation of Hume by other means. (The work of J. L. Austin for instance is a detailed and brilliant exorcism of the notion of the sense-impression. Yet by substituting an impersonal language-world for the old impersonal atom-world of Hume and Russell he in a way 'saves' the latter.) What the philosopher is trying to characterize, indeed to justify, is still the idea of an impersonal world of facts: the hard objective world out of which the will leaps into a position of isolation. What defines and constitutes fact has been removed from one place to another, but the radical idea of 'fact' remains much the same. Logic (impersonal rules) here obliges science with a philosophical model.

What makes difficulties for this model is the conception of persons or individuals, a conception inseparable from morality. The whole vocabulary, so profoundly familiar to us, of 'appearance' and 'reality', whether as used by the old British empiricists or by modern empiricism, is blunt and crude when applied to the human individual. Consider for instance the case of a man trying privately to determine whether something which he 'feels' is repentance or not. Of course this investigation is subject to some public rules, otherwise it would not be this investigation: and there could be doubts or disputes about whether it is this investigation. But these apart, the activity in question must remain a highly personal one upon which the *prise* of 'the impersonal world of language' is to say the least problematic: or rather it is an activity which puts in question the existence of such an impersonal world. Here an individual is making a specialized personal *use* of a concept. Of course he derives the concept initially from his surroundings; but he takes it away into his privacy. Concepts of this sort lend themselves to such uses; and what use is made of them is partly a function of the user's history. Hume and Kant, the two patron saints of modern philosophy, abhor history, each in his own way, and abhor the particular notion of privacy which history implies. A certain conception of logic and a certain conception of science also abhor history.

But once the historical individual is 'let in' a number of things have to be said with a difference. The idea of 'objective reality', for instance, undergoes important modifications when it is to be understood, not in relation to 'the world described by science', but in relation to the progressing life of a person. The active 'reassessing' and 'redefining' which is a main characteristic of live personality often suggests and demands a checking procedure which is a function of an individual history. Repentance may mean something different to an individual at different times in his life, and what it fully means is a part of this life and cannot be understood except in context.

There is of course a 'science' which concerns itself especially with the history of the individual: psychoanalysis. And with a determination at all costs not to part company with a scientific conception of 'the objective' it is to psycho-analysis that Professor Hampshire finally appeals: he very properly lets in the historical individual, but hopes to keep him by this means upon a lead. Hampshire reads in an impersonal background to the individual's checking procedure with the help of the notion of an ideal analysis. The analyst is pictured as somehow 'there', as the ultimate competent observer playing the part of the eye of God. Hampshire allows that it is possible in theory though not in practice to 'approach complete explanations of inclination and behaviour in any individual case through an interminable analysis'. But why should some unspecified psychoanalyst be the measure of all things? Psychoanalysis is a muddled embryonic science, and even if it were not there is no argument that I know of that can show us that we have got to treat its concepts as fundamental. The notion of an 'ideal analysis' is a misleading one. There is no existing series the extension of which could lead to such an ideal. This is a *moral* question; and what is at stake here is the liberation of morality, and of philosophy as a study of human nature, from the domination of science: or rather from the domination of inexact ideas of science which haunt philosophers and other thinkers. Because of the lack until fairly recently of any clear distinction between science and philosophy this issue has never presented itself so vividly before. Philosophy in the past has played the game of science partly because it thought it was science.

Existentialism, in both its Continental and its Anglo-Saxon versions, is an attempt to solve the problem without really facing it: to solve it by attributing to the individual an empty lonely freedom, a freedom, if he wishes, to 'fly in the face of the facts'. What it pictures is indeed the fearful solitude of the individual marooned upon a tiny island in the middle of a sea of scientific facts, and morality escaping from science only by a wild leap of the will. But our situation is not like this. To put it simply and in terms of the example which we have considered of M and her daughter-in-law: even if M were given a full psychoanalytical explanation of her conduct to D she need not be confined by such an explanation. This is not just because M has a senseless petulant freedom which enables her to be blind, nor is it just because (the more subtle view favoured by Hampshire) she is then enabled to redeploy her psychic forces on a ground of greater knowledge. It is because M is not forced to adopt these concepts at all, in preference say to any particular set of moral or religious concepts. Science can instruct morality at certain points and can change its direction, but it cannot contain morality, nor ergo moral philosophy. The importance of this issue can more easily be ignored by a philosophy which divorces freedom and knowledge, and leaves knowledge (via an uncriticized idea of 'impersonal reasons') in the domain of science. But M's independence of science and of the 'world of facts' which empiricist philosophy has created in the scientific image rests not simply in her moving will but in her seeing knowing mind. Moral concepts do not move about within a hard world set up by science and logic. They set up, for different purposes, a different world.

Let me try now to explain more positively what it is about moral concepts which puts them entirely out of relation with the behaviourist view with its genetic explanation of mental phenomena. I want here to connect two ideas: the idea of the individual and the idea of perfection. Love is knowledge of the individual. M confronted with D has an endless task. Moral tasks are characteristically endless not only because 'within', as it were, a given concept our efforts are imperfect, but also because as we move and as we look our concepts themselves are changing. To speak here of an inevitable imperfection, or of an ideal limit of love or knowledge which always recedes, may be taken as a reference to our 'fallen' human condition, but this need be given no special dogmatic sense. Since we are neither angels nor animals but human individuals, our dealings with each other have this aspect; and this may be regarded as an empirical fact or, by those who favour such terminology, as a synthetic *a priori* truth.

The entry into a mental concept of the notion of an ideal limit destroys the genetic analysis of its meaning. (Hampshire allowed the idea of perfection to touch one concept only, that of intention: but he tried to save this concept from morality by making the ideal limit a scientific one.) Let us see how this is. Is 'love' a mental concept, and if so can it be analysed genetically? No doubt Mary's little lamb loved Mary, that is it followed her to school; and in some sense of 'learn' we might well learn the concept, the word, in that context. But with such a concept that is not the end of the matter. (Nor indeed the beginning either.) Words may mislead us here since words are often stable while concepts alter; we have a different image of courage at forty from that which we had at twenty. A deepening process, at any rate an altering and complicating process, takes place. There are two senses of 'knowing what a word means', one connected with ordinary language and the other very much less so. Knowledge of a value concept is something to be understood, as it were, in depth, and not in terms of switching on to some given impersonal network. Moreover, if morality is essentially connected with change and progress, we cannot be as democratic about it as some philosophers would like to think. We do not simply, through being rational and knowing ordinary language, 'know' the meaning of all necessary moral words. We may have to learn the meaning; and since we are human historical individuals the movement of understanding is onward into increasing privacy, in the direction of the ideal limit, and not back towards a genesis in the rulings of an impersonal public language.

None of what I am saying here is particularly new: similar things have been said by philosophers from Plato onward; and appear as commonplaces of the Christian ethic, whose centre is an individual. To come nearer home in the Platonic tradition, the present dispute is reminiscent of the old arguments about abstract and concrete universals. My view might be put by saying: moral terms must be treated as concrete universals. And if someone at this point were to say, well, why stop at moral concepts, why not claim that all universals are concrete, I would reply, why not indeed? Why not consider red as an ideal end-point, as a concept infinitely to be learned, as an individual object of love? A painter might say, 'You don't know what "red" means.' This would be, by a counter-attack, to bring the idea of value, which has been driven by science and logic into a corner, back to cover the whole field of knowledge. But this would be part of a different argument and is not my concern here. Perhaps all concepts could be considered in this way: all I am now arguing is that some concepts must be.

In suggesting that the central concept of morality is 'the individual' thought of as knowable by love, thought of in the light of the command, 'Be ye therefore perfect', I am not, in spite of the philosophical backing which I might here resort to, suggesting anything in the least esoteric. In fact this would, to the ordinary person, be a very much more familiar image than the existentialist one. We ordinarily conceive of and apprehend goodness in terms of virtues which belong to a continuous fabric of being. And it is just the historical, individual, nature of the virtues as actually exemplified which makes it difficult to learn goodness from another person. It is all very well to say that 'to copy a right action is to act rightly' (Hampshire, *Logic and Appreciation*), but what is the form which I am supposed to copy? It is a truism of recent philosophy that this operation of discerning the form is fairly easy, that rationality in this simple sense is a going concern. And of course for certain conventional purposes it is. But it is characteristic of morals that one cannot rest entirely at the conventional level, and that in some ways one ought not to.

We might consider in this context the ambiguity of Kant's position in the *Grundlegung*, where he tells us that when confronted with the person of Christ we must turn back to the pattern of rationality in our own bosoms and decide whether or not we approve of the man we see. Kant is often claimed as a backer of the existentialist view: and these words may readily be taken to advocate that return to self, that concern with the purity of the solitary will, which is favoured by all brands of existentialism. Here I stand alone, in total responsibility and freedom, and can only properly and responsibly do what is intelligible to me, what I can do with a clear intention. But it must be remembered that Kant was a 'metaphysical naturalist' and not an existentialist. Reason itself is for him an ideal limit: indeed his term 'Idea of Reason' expresses precisely that endless aspiration to perfection which is characteristic of moral activity. His is not the 'achieved' or 'given' reason which belongs with 'ordinary language' and convention, nor is his man on the other hand totally unguided and alone. There exists a moral reality, a real though infinitely distant standard: the difficulties of understanding and imitating remain. And in a way it is perhaps a matter of tactics and temperament whether we should look at Christ or at Reason. Kant was especially impressed by the dangers of blind obedience to a person or an institution. But there are (as the history of existentialism shows) just as many dangers attaching to the ambiguous idea of finding the ideal in one's own bosom. The argument for looking outward at Christ and not inward at Reason is that self is such a dazzling object that if one looks there one may see nothing else. But as I say, so long as the gaze is directed upon the ideal the exact formulation will be a matter of history and tactics in a sense which is not rigidly determined by religious dogma, and understanding of the ideal will be partial in any case. Where virtue is concerned we often apprehend more than we clearly understand and grow by looking.

Let me suggest in more detail how I think this process actually happens. This will I hope enable me to clarify the status of the view I hold and to relate it to linguistic philosophy in particular. I have spoken of a process of deepening or complicating, a process of learning, a progress, which may take place in moral concepts in the dimension which they possess in virtue of their relation to an ideal limit. In describing the example of M and her daughter-in-law I drew attention to the important part played by the normative-descriptive words, the specialized or secondary value words. (Such as 'vulgar', 'spontaneous', etc.) By means of these words there takes place what we might call 'the siege of the individual by concepts'. Uses of such words are both instruments and symptoms of learning. Learning takes place when such words are used, either aloud or privately, in the context of particular acts of attention. (M attending to D.) This is a point to be emphasized. That words are not timeless, that word-utterances are historical occasions, has been noted by some philosophers for some purposes. (Strawson notes it when attacking the Theory of Descriptions.) But the full implications of this fact, with its consequences for the would-be timeless image of reason, have not, in our modern philosophy, been fully drawn. As Plato observes at the end of the *Phaedrus*, words themselves do not contain wisdom. Words said to particular individuals at particular times may occasion wisdom. Words, moreover, have both spatio-temporal and conceptual contexts. We learn through attending to contexts, vocabulary develops through close attention to objects, and we can only understand others if we can to some extent share their contexts. (Often we cannot.) Uses of words by persons grouped round a common object is a central and vital human activity. The art critic can help us if we are in the presence of the same object and if we know something about his scheme of concepts. Both contexts are relevant to our ability to move towards 'seeing more', towards 'seeing what he sees'. Here, as so often, an aesthetic analogy is helpful for morals. M could be helped by someone who both knew D and whose conceptual scheme M could understand or in that context begin to understand. Progress in understanding of a scheme of concepts often takes place as we listen to normative-descriptive talk in the presence of a common object. I have been speaking, in relation to our example, of progress or change for the better, but of course such change (and this is more commonly to be observed) may also be for the worse. Everyday conversation is not necessarily a morally neutral activity and certain ways of describing people can be corrupting and wrong. A smart set of concepts may be a most efficient instrument of corruption. It is especially characteristic of normative words, both desirable and undesirable, to belong to sets or patterns without an appreciation of which they cannot be understood. If a critic tells us that a picture has 'functional colour' or 'significant form' we need to know not only the picture but also something about his general theory in order to understand the remark. Similarly, if M says D is 'common', although the term does not belong to a technical vocabulary, this use of it can only be fully understood if we know not only D but M.

This dependence of language upon contexts of attention has consequences. Language is far more idiosyncratic than has been admitted. Reasons are not necessarily and qua reasons public. They may be reasons for a very few, and none the worse for that. 'I can't explain. You'd have to know her.' If the common object is lacking, communication may break down and the same words may occasion different results in different hearers. This may seem on reflection very obvious; but philosophy is often a matter of finding a suitable context in which to say the obvious. Human beings are obscure to each other, in certain respects which are particularly relevant to morality, unless they are mutual objects of attention or have common objects of attention, since this affects the degree of elaboration of a common vocabulary. We develop language in the context of looking: the metaphor of vision again. The notion of privileged access to inner events has been held morally suspect because, among other things, it would separate people from 'the ordinary world of rational argument'. But the unavoidable contextual privacy of language already does this, and except at a very simple and conventional level of communication there is no such ordinary world. This conclusion is feared and avoided by many moralists because it seems inimical to the operation of reason and because reason is construed on a scientific model. Scientific language tries to be impersonal and exact and yet accessible for purposes of teamwork; and the degree of accessibility can be decided in relation to definite practical goals. Moral language which relates to a reality infinitely more complex and various than that of science is often unavoidably idiosyncratic and inaccessible.

Words are the most subtle symbols which we possess and our human fabric depends on them. The living and radical nature of language is something which we forget at our peril. It is totally misleading to speak, for instance, of 'two cultures', one literary-humane and the other scientific, as if these were of equal status. There is only one culture, of which science, so interesting and so dangerous, is now an important part. But the most essential and fundamental aspect of culture is the study of literature, since this is an education in how to picture and understand human situations. We are men and we are moral agents before we are scientists, and the place of science in human life must be discussed in *words*. This is why it is and always will be more important to know about Shakespeare than to know about any scientist: and if there is a 'Shakespeare of science' his name is Aristotle.

I have used the word 'attention', which I borrow from Simone Weil, to express the idea of a just and loving gaze directed upon an individual reality. I believe this to be the characteristic and proper mark of the active moral agent. 'Characteristic' and 'proper' suggest in turn a logical and a normative claim; and I shall discuss below how far what I say is to be taken as recommendation and how far as description. In any case a theory, whether normative or logical, is the more attractive the more it explains, the more its structure may be seen as underlying things which are familiar to us in ordinary life. I want now to go on to argue that the view I am suggesting offers a more satisfactory account of human freedom than does the existential-ist view. I have classified together as existentialist both philo-sophers such as Sartre who claim the title, and philosophers such as Hampshire, Hare, Ayer, who do not. Characteristic of both is the identification of the true person with the empty choosing will, and the corresponding emphasis upon the idea of move-ment rather than vision. This emphasis will go with the anti-naturalistic bias of existentialism. There is no point in talking of 'moral seeing' since there is nothing morally to see. There is no moral vision. There is only the ordinary world which is seen with ordinary vision, and there is the will that moves within it. What may be called the Kantian wing and the Surrealist wing of existentialism may be distinguished by the degree of their interest in reasons for action, which diminishes to nothing at the Surrealist end.

Our British philosophers are of course very interested in reasons, emphasizing, as I have said, the accessibility, the non-esoteric nature of moral reasoning. But the production of such reasons, it is argued (and this is indeed the point of emphasizing their impersonal character), does not in any way connect or tie the agent to the world or to special personal contexts within the world. He freely chooses his reasons in terms of, and after sur-veying, the ordinary facts which lie open to everyone: and he acts. This operation, it is argued, is the exercise of freedom. This image of man as a highly conscious self-contained being is offered by some philosophers as a donné and by others, e.g. Hampshire, as a norm; although Hampshire is careful to give the norm a scientific background.

Let us now ask quite simply if this is realistic, if this is what, in our experience, moral choice is like. It might seem at first that the existentialists have an advantage in that they do account for a peculiar feature of moral choice, which is the strange emptiness which often occurs at the moment of choosing. Of course choices happen at various levels of consciousness, importance, and difficulty. In a simple easy unimportant choice there is no need to regard 'what goes on' as anything beyond the obvious sequence of reason, decision, action, or just reason, action; and such choices may properly be regarded as 'impersonal'. 'Shall I go? Oh yes, I promised to.' I receive my bill and I pay it. But difficult and painful choices often present this experience of void of which so much has been made: this sense of not being determined by the reasons. This sensation is hailed with delight by both wings of existentialism. The Kantian wing claims it as showing that we are free in relation to the reasons and the Surrealist wing claims it as showing that there are no reasons. Indeed this experience of emptiness seems perfectly to verify the notion that freedom is simply the movement of the lonely will. Choice is outward movement since there is nothing else there for it to be.

But is this the case, and ought we really to be so pleased about this experience? A more sombre note concerning it is struck at one point by Sartre, who on this problem veers wildly between Kantianism and Surrealism. *Quand je délibère les jeux sont faits.* If we are so strangely separate from the world at moments of choice are we really choosing at all, are we right indeed to identify *ourselves* with this giddy empty will? (Hampshire: 'I identify myself with my will.') In a reaction of thought which is never far from the minds of more extreme existentialists (Dostoevsky for instance), one may turn here towards determinism, towards fatalism, towards regarding freedom as a complete illusion. When I deliberate the die is already cast. Forces within me which are dark to me have already made the decision.

This view is if anything less attractive and less realistic than the other one. Do we really have to choose between an image of total freedom and an image of total determinism? Can we not give a more balanced and illuminating account of the matter? I suggest we can if we simply introduce into the picture the idea of *attention*, or looking, of which I was speaking above. I can only choose within the world I can *see*, in the moral sense of 'see' which implies that clear vision is a result of moral imagination and moral effort. There is also of course 'distorted vision', and the word 'reality' here inevitably appears as a normative word. When M is just and loving she sees D as she really is. One is often compelled almost automatically by what one *can* see. If we ignore the prior work of attention and notice only the emptiness of the moment of choice we are likely to identify freedom with the outward movement since there is nothing else to identify it with. But if we consider what the work of attention is like, how continuously it goes on, and how imperceptibly it builds up structures of value round about us, we shall not be surprised that at crucial moments of choice most of the business of choosing is already over. This does not imply that we are not free, certainly not. But it implies that the exercise of our freedom is a small piecemeal business which goes on all the time and not a grandiose leaping about unimpeded at important moments. The moral life, on this view, is something that goes on continually, not something that is switched off in between the occurrence of explicit moral choices. What happens in between such choices is indeed what is crucial. I would like on the whole to use the word 'attention' as a good word and use some more general term like 'looking' as the neutral word. Of course psychic energy flows, and more readily flows, into building up convincingly coherent but false pictures of the world, complete with systematic vocabulary. (M seeing D as pert-common-juvenile, etc.) Attention is the effort to counteract such states of illusion.

On this view we are certainly in a sense less free than we are pictured as being on the other view, in that the latter presents a condition of perfect freedom as being either our unavoidable fate (the Surrealists) or our conceivably attainable goal (the Kantians). Freedom for Hampshire is a matter of having crystal-clear intentions. But on the view which I suggest, which connects morality with attention to individuals, human individuals or individual realities of other kinds, the struggle and the progress is something more obscure, more historically conditioned, and usually less clearly conscious. Freedom, itself a moral concept and not just a prerequisite of morality, cannot here be separated from the idea of knowledge. That of which it is knowledge, that 'reality' which we are so naturally led to think of as revealed by just 'attention', can of course, given the variety of human personality and situation, only be thought of as 'one', as a single object for all men, in some very remote and ideal sense. It is a deep paradox of moral philosophy that almost all philosophers have been led in one way or another to picture goodness as knowledge: and yet to show this in any sort of detail, to show 'reality' as 'one', seems to involve an improper prejudging of some moral issue. An acute consciousness of this latter difficulty has indeed made it seem axiomatic to recent philosophers that 'naturalism is a fallacy'. But I would suggest that at the level of serious common sense and of an ordinary non-philosophical reflection about the nature of morals it is perfectly obvious that goodness is connected with knowledge: not with impersonal quasi-scientific knowledge of the ordinary world, whatever that may be, but with a refined and honest perception of what is really the case, a patient and just discernment and exploration of what confronts one, which is the result not simply of opening one's eyes but of a certainly perfectly familiar kind of moral discipline.

What then of the 'void', the experience of *Angst* of which the existentialists have told us so much? If it cannot be understood in their sense as an experience of pure freedom, what is it, and does it really occur at all? Perhaps there are several different conditions involved here. But the central one, the heart of the concept, I think I would describe rather as a kind of fright which the conscious will feels when it apprehends the strength and direction of the personality which is not under its immediate control. Innumerable 'lookings' have discovered and explored a world which is now (for better or worse) *compulsively* present to the will in a particular situation, and the will is dismayed by the feeling that it ought now to be everything and in fact is not. *Angst* may occur where there is any felt discrepancy between personality and ideals. Perhaps very simple people escape it and some civilizations have not experienced it at all. Extreme *Angst*, in the popular modern form, is a disease or addiction of those who are passionately convinced that personality resides solely in the conscious omnipotent will: and in so far as this conviction is wrong the condition partakes of illusion. It is obviously, in practice, a delicate moral problem to decide how far the will can coerce the formed personality (*move* in a world it cannot *see*) without merely occasioning disaster. The concept of *Angst* should of course be carefully distinguished from its ancestor, Kant's *Achtung*, in which dismay at the frailty of the will is combined with an inspiring awareness of the reality which the will is drawn by (despair at the sensuous will, joy in the rational will). The loss of that awareness, or that faith, produces *Angst*, which is properly a condition of sober alarm. Those who are, or attempt to be, exhilarated by *Angst*, that is by the mere impotence of the will and its lack of connection with the personality, are, as I have suggested above, in danger of falling into fatalism or sheer irresponsibility.

The place of choice is certainly a different one if we think in terms of a world which is *compulsively* present to the will, and the discernment and exploration of which is a slow business. Moral change and moral achievement are slow; we are not free in the sense of being able suddenly to alter ourselves since we cannot suddenly alter what we can see and ergo what we desire and are compelled by. In a way, explicit choice seems now less important: less decisive (since much of the 'decision' lies elsewhere) and less obviously something to be 'cultivated'. If I attend properly I will have no choices and this is the ultimate condition to be aimed at. This is in a way the reverse of Hampshire's picture, where our efforts are supposed to be directed to increasing our freedom by conceptualizing as many different possibilities of action as possible: having as many goods as possible in the shop. The ideal situation, on the contrary, is rather to be represented as a kind of 'necessity'. This is something of which saints speak and which any artist will readily understand. The idea of a patient, loving regard, directed upon a person, a thing, a situation, presents the will not as unimpeded movement but as something very much more like 'obedience'.

Will and reason then are not entirely separate faculties in the moral agent. Will continually influences belief; for better or worse, and is ideally able to influence it through a sustained attention to reality. This is what Simone Weil means when she says that 'will is obedience not resolution'. As moral agents we have to try to see justly, to overcome prejudice, to avoid temptation, to control and curb imagination, to direct reflection. Man is not a combination of an impersonal rational thinker and a personal will. He is a unified being who sees, and who desires in accordance with what he sees, and who has some continual slight control over the direction and focus of his vision. There is nothing, I think, in the foreground of this picture which is unfamiliar to the ordinary person. Philosophical difficulties may arise if we try to give any single organized background sense to the normative word 'reality'. But this word may be used as a philosophical term provided its limitations are understood. What is real may be 'non-empirical' without being in the grand sense systematic. In particular situations 'reality' as that which is revealed to the patient eye of love is an idea entirely comprehensible to the ordinary person. M knows what she is doing when she tries to be just to D, and we know what she is doing too.

I said that any artist would appreciate the notion of ill as obedience to reality, an obedience which ideally teaches a position where there is no choice. One of the great merits of the moral psychology which I am proposing is that it does not contrast art and morals, but shows them to be two aspects of a single struggle. The existentialist-behaviourist view could give no satisfactory account of art: it was seen as a quasi-play activity, gratuitous, 'for its own sake' (the familiar Kantian-Bloomsbury slogan), a sort of by-product of our failure to be entirely rational. Such a view of art is of course intolerable. In one of those important movements of return from philosophical theory to simple things which we are certain of, we must come back to what we know about great art and about the moral insight which it contains and the moral achievement which it represents. Goodness and beauty are not to be contrasted, but are largely part of the same structure. Plato, who tells us that beauty is the only spiritual thing which we love immediately by nature, treats the beautiful as an introductory section of the good. So that aesthetic situations are not so much analogies of morals as cases of morals. Virtue is *au fond* the same in the artist as in the good man in that it is a selfless attention to nature: something which is easy to name but very hard to achieve. Artists who have reflected have frequently given expression to this idea. (For instance, Rilke praising Cézanne speaks of a 'consuming of love in anonymous work'. Letter to Clara Rilke, 13 October 1907.)

Since the existentialist-behaviourist view wished to conceive of will as pure movement separated from reason and to deprive reason of the use of normative words (since it was to be 'objective'), the moral agent so envisaged could get along, was indeed almost forced to get along, with only the most empty and general moral terms such as 'good' and 'right'. The empty moral words correspond here to the emptiness of the will. If the will is to be totally free the world it moves in must be devoid of normative characteristics, so that morality can reside entirely in the pointer of pure choice. On my view it might be said that, *per contra*, the primary general words could be dispensed with entirely and all moral work could be done by the secondary specialized words. If we picture the agent as compelled by obedience to the reality he can see, he will not be saying 'This is right', i.e., 'I choose to do this', he will be saying 'This is A B C D' (normative-descriptive words), and action will follow naturally. As the empty choice will not occur the empty word will not be needed. It would however be far from my intention to demote or dispense with the term 'good': but rather to restore to it the dignity and authority which it possessed before Moore appeared on the scene. I have spoken of efforts of attention directed upon individuals and of obedience to reality as an exercise of love, and have suggested that 'reality' and 'individual' present themselves to us in moral contexts as ideal end-points or Ideas of Reason. This surely is the place where the concept of good lives. 'Good': 'Real': 'Love'. These words are closely connected. And here we retrieve the deep sense of the indefinability of good, which has been given a trivial sense in recent philosophy. Good is indefinable not for the reasons offered by Moore's successors, but because of the infinite difficulty of the task of apprehending a magnetic but inexhaustible reality. Moore was in a way nearer the truth than he realized when he tried to say both that Good was there and that one could say nothing of what it essentially was. If apprehension of good is apprehension of the individual and the real, then good partakes of the infinite elusive character of reality.

I have several times indicated that the image which I am offering should be thought of as a general metaphysical background to morals and not as a formula which can be illuminatingly introduced into any and every moral act. There exists, so far as I know, no formula of the latter kind. We are not always the individual in pursuit of the individual, we are not always responding to the magnetic pull of the idea of perfection. Often, for instance when we pay our bills or perform other small everyday acts, we are just 'anybody' doing what is proper or making simple choices for ordinary public reasons; and this is the situation which some philosophers have chosen exclusively to analyse. Furthermore, I am well aware of the moral dangers of the idea of morality as something which engages the whole person and which may lead to specialized and esoteric vision and language. Give and take between the private and the public levels of morality is often of advantage to both and indeed is normally unavoidable. In fact the 'conventional' level is often not so simple as it seems, and the quaintly phrased hymn which I sang in my childhood, 'Who sweeps a room as for Thy laws makes that and the action fine', was not talking foolishly. The task of attention goes on all the time and at apparently empty and everyday moments we are 'looking', making those little peering efforts of imagination which have such important cumulative results.

I would not be understood, either, as suggesting that insight or pureness of heart are more important than action: the thing which philosophers feared Moore for implying. Overt actions are perfectly obviously important in themselves, and important too because they are the indispensable pivot and spur of the inner scene. The inner, in this sense, cannot do without the outer. I do not mean only that outer rituals make places for inner experiences; but also that an overt action can release psychic energies which can be released in no other way. We often receive an unforeseen reward for a fumbling half-hearted act: a place for the idea of grace. I have suggested that we have to accept a darker, less fully conscious, less steadily rational image of the dynamics of the human personality. With this dark entity behind us we may sometimes decide to act abstractly by rule, to ignore vision and the compulsive energy derived from it; and we may find that as a result both energy and vision are unexpectedly given. To decide when to attempt such leaps is one of the most difficult of moral problems. But if we do leap ahead of what we know we still have to try to catch up. Will cannot run very far ahead of knowledge, and attention is our daily bread.

Of course what I have been offering here is not and does not pretend to be a 'neutral logical analysis' of what moral agents or moral terms are like. The picture offered by, e.g., Hampshire is of course not neutral either, as he admits in parenthesis. (*Thought and Action*, Chapter Two.) 'A decision has to be made between two conceptions of personality. . . . It may be that in a society in which a man's theoretical opinions and religious beliefs were held to be supremely important, a man's beliefs would be considered as much part of his responsibility as his behaviour to other men.' And he contrasts this with 'a utilitarian culture'. Hampshire speaks here of a 'decision'; and there is always an existentialist 'short way' with any rival theory: to say, 'You use that picture, but you *choose* to use it.' This is to make the existentialist picture the ultimate one. I would wish to exclude any such undercutting of my theory. To say that it is a normative theory is not to say that it is an object of free choice: modern philosophy has equated these ideas but this is just the equation I am objecting to. I offer frankly a sketch of a metaphysical theory, a kind of inconclusive non-dogmatic naturalism, which has the circularity of definition characteristic of such theories. The rival theory is similarly circular; and as I have explained I do not find that its radical arguments convincingly establish its sweeping moral and psychological conclusions.

Philosophers have always been trying to picture the human soul, and since morality needs such pictures and as science is, as I have argued, in no position to coerce morality, there seems no reason why philosophers should not go on attempting to fill in a systematic explanatory background to our ordinary moral life. Hampshire said, and I quoted this at the start, that 'it is the constructive task of the philosophy of mind to provide a set of terms in which ultimate judgements of value can be very clearly stated'. I would put what I think is much the same task in terms of the provision of rich and fertile conceptual schemes which help us to reflect upon and understand the nature of moral progress and moral failure and the reasons for the divergence of one moral temperament from another. And I would wish to make my theory undercut its existentialist rivals by suggesting that it is possible in terms of the former to explain why people are obsessed with the latter, but not vice versa. In any case, the sketch which I have offered, a footnote in a great and familiar philosophical tradition, must be judged by its power to connect, to illuminate, to explain, and to make new and fruitful places for reflection.

2

ON 'GOD' AND 'GOOD'

To do philosophy is to explore one's own temperament, and yet at the same time to attempt to discover the truth. It seems to me that there is a void in present-day moral philosophy. Areas peripheral to philosophy expand (psychology, political and social theory) or collapse (religion) without philosophy being able in the one case to encounter, and in the other case to rescue, the values involved. A working philosophical psychology is needed which can at least attempt to connect modern psychological terminology with a terminology concerned with virtue. We need a moral philosophy which can speak significantly of Freud and Marx, and out of which aesthetic and political views can be generated. We need a moral philosophy in which the concept of love, so rarely mentioned now by philosophers, can once again be made central.

It will be said, we have got a working philosophy, and one which is the proper heir to the past of European philosophy: existentialism. This philosophy does so far pervade the scene that philosophers, many linguistic analysts for instance, who would not claim the name, do in fact work with existentialist concepts. I shall argue that existentialism is not, and cannot by tinkering be made, the philosophy we need. Although it is indeed the heir of the past, it is (it seems to me) an unrealistic and over-optimistic doctrine and the purveyor of certain false values. This is more obviously true of flimsier creeds, such as 'humanism', with which people might now attempt to fill the philosophical void.

The great merit of existentialism is that it at least professes and tries to be a philosophy one could live by. Kierkegaard described the Hegelian system as a grand palace set up by someone who then lived in a hovel or at best in the porter's lodge. A moral philosophy should be inhabited. Existentialism has shown itself capable of becoming a popular philosophy and of getting into the minds of those (e.g. Oxford philosophers) who have not sought it and may even be unconscious of its presence. However, although it can certainly inspire action, it seems to me to do so by a sort of romantic provocation rather than by its truth; and its pointers are often pointing in the wrong direction. Wittgenstein claimed that he brought the Cartesian era in philosophy to an end. Moral philosophy of an existentialist type is still Cartesian and egocentric. Briefly put, our picture of ourselves has become too grand, we have isolated, and identified ourselves with, an unrealistic conception of will, we have lost the vision of a reality separate from ourselves, and we have no adequate conception of original sin. Kierkegaard rightly observed that 'an ethic which ignores sin is an altogether useless science', although he also added, 'but if it recognizes sin it is *eo ipso* beyond its sphere'.

Kant believed in Reason and Hegel believed in History, and for both this was a form of a belief in an external reality. Modern thinkers who believe in neither, but who remain within the tradition, are left with a denuded self whose only virtues are freedom, or at best sincerity, or, in the case of the British philosophers, an everyday reasonableness. Philosophy, on its other fronts, has been busy dismantling the old substantial picture of the 'self', and ethics has not proved able to rethink this concept for moral purposes. The moral agent then is pictured as an isolated principle of will, or burrowing pinpoint of consciousness, inside, or beside, a lump of being which has been handed over to other disciplines, such as psychology or sociology. On the one hand a Luciferian philosophy of adventures of the will, and on the other natural science. Moral philosophy, and indeed morals, are thus undefended against an irresponsible and undirected self-assertion which goes easily hand in hand with some brand of pseudo-scientific determinism. An unexamined sense of the strength of the machine is combined with an illusion of leaping out of it. The younger Sartre, and many British moral philosophers, represent this last dry distilment of Kant's views of the world. The study of motivation is surrendered to empirical science: will takes the place of the complex of motives and also of the complex of virtues.

The history of British philosophy since Moore represents intensively in miniature the special dilemmas of modern ethics. Empiricism, especially in the form given to it by Russell, and later by Wittgenstein, thrust ethic almost out of philosophy. Moral judgments were not factual, or truthful, and had no place in the world of the *Tractatus*. Moore, although he himself held a curious metaphysic of 'moral facts', set the tone when he told us that we must carefully distinguish the question 'What things are good?' from the question 'What does "good" mean?' The answer to the latter question concerned the will. Good was indefinable (naturalism was a fallacy) because any offered good could be scrutinized by any individual by a 'stepping back' movement. This form of Kantianism still retains its appeal. Wittgenstein had attacked the idea of the Cartesian ego or substantial self and Ryle and others had developed the attack. A study of 'ordinary language' claimed (often rightly) to solve piecemeal problems in epistemology which had formerly been discussed in terms of the activities or faculties of a 'self'. (See John Austin's book on certain problems of perception, *Sense and Sensibilia*.)

Ethics took its place in this scene. After puerile attempts to classify moral statements as exclamations or expressions of emotion, a more sophisticated neo-Kantianism with a utilitarian atmosphere has been developed. The idea of the agent as a privileged centre of will (for ever capable of 'stepping back') is retained, but, since the old-fashioned 'self' no longer clothes him he appears as an isolated will operating with the concepts of 'ordinary language', so far as the field of morals is concerned. (It is interesting that although Wittgenstein's work has suggested this picture to others, he himself never used it.) Thus the will, and the psyche as an object of science, are isolated from each other and from the rest of philosophy. The cult of ordinary language goes with the claim to be neutral. Previous moral philosophers told us what we ought to do, that is they tried to answer both of Moore's questions. Linguistic analysis claims simply to give a philosophical description of the human phenomenon of morality, without making any moral judgments. In fact the resulting picture of human conduct has a clear moral bias. The merits of linguistic analytical man are freedom (in the sense of detachment, rationality), responsibility, self-awareness, sincerity, and a lot of utilitarian common sense. There is of course no mention of sin, and no mention of love. Marxism is ignored, and there is on the whole no attempt at a *rapprochement* with psychology, although Professor Hampshire does try to develop the idea of self-awareness towards an ideal end-point by conceiving of 'the perfect psychoanalysis' which would make us perfectly self-aware and so perfectly detached and free.

Linguistic analysis of course poses for ethics the question of its relation with metaphysics. Can ethics be a form of empiricism? Many philosophers in the Oxford and Cambridge tradition would say yes. It is certainly a great merit of this tradition, and one which I would not wish to lose sight of, that it attacks every form of spurious unity. It is the traditional inspiration of the philosopher, but also his traditional vice, to believe that all is one. Wittgenstein says 'Let's see.' Sometimes problems turn out to be quite unconnected with each other, and demand types of solution which are not themselves closely related in any system. Perhaps it is a matter of temperament whether or not one is convinced that all is one. (My own temperament inclines to monism.) But let us postpone the question of whether, if we reject the relaxed empirical ethics of the British tradition (a cheerful amalgam of Hume, Kant and Mill), and if we reject, too, the more formal existentialist systems, we wish to replace these with something which would have to be called a metaphysical theory. Let me now simply suggest ways in which I take the prevalent and popular picture to be unrealistic. In doing this my debt to Simone Weil will become evident.

Much of contemporary moral philosophy appears both unambitious and optimistic. Unambitious optimism is of course part of the Anglo-Saxon tradition; and it is also not surprising that a philosophy which analyses moral concepts on the basis of ordinary language should present a relaxed picture of a mediocre achievement. I think the charge is also true, though contrary to some appearances, of existentialism. An authentic mode of existence is presented as attainable by intelligence and force of will. The atmosphere is invigorating and tends to produce self-satisfaction in the reader, who feels himself to be a member of the élite, addressed by another one. Contempt for the ordinary human condition, together with a conviction of personal salvation, saves the writer from real pessimism. His gloom is superficial and conceals elation. (I think this to be true in different ways of both Sartre and Heidegger, though I am never too sure of having understood the latter.) Such attitudes contrast with the vanishing images of Christian theology which represented goodness as almost impossibly difficult, and sin as almost insuperable and certainly as a universal condition.

Yet modern psychology has provided us with what might be called a doctrine of original sin, a doctrine which most philosophers either deny (Sartre), ignore (Oxford and Cambridge), or attempt to render innocuous (Hampshire). When I speak in this context of modern psychology I mean primarily the work of Freud. I am not a 'Freudian' and the truth of this or that particular view of Freud does not here concern me, but it seems clear that Freud made an important discovery about the human mind and that he remains still the greatest scientist in the field which he opened. One may say that what he presents us with is a realistic and detailed picture of the fallen man. If we take the general outline of this picture seriously, and at the same time wish to do moral philosophy, we shall have to revise the current conceptions of will and motive very considerably. What seems to me, for these purposes, true and important in Freudian theory is as follows. Freud takes a thoroughly pessimistic view of human nature. He sees the psyche as an egocentric system of quasi-mechanical energy, largely determined by its own individual history, whose natural attachments are sexual, ambiguous, and hard for the subject to understand or control. Introspection reveals only the deep tissue of ambivalent motive, and fantasy is a stronger force than reason. Objectivity and unselfishness are not natural to human beings.

Of course Freud is saying these things in the context of a scientific therapy which aims not at making people good but at making them workable. If a moral philosopher says such things he must justify them not with scientific arguments but with arguments appropriate to philosophy; and in fact if he does say such things he will not be saying anything very new, since partially similar views have been expressed before in philosophy, as far back as Plato. It is important to look at Freud and his successors because they can give us more information about a mechanism the general nature of which we may discern without the help of science; and also because the ignoring of psychology may be a source of confusion. Some philosophers (e.g. Sartre) regard traditional psycho-analytical theory as a form of determinism and are prepared to deny it at all levels, and philosophers who ignore it often do so as part of an easy surrender to science of aspects of the mind which ought to interest them. But determinism as a total philosophical theory is not the enemy. Determinism as a philosophical theory is quite unproven, and it can be argued that it is not possible in principle to translate propositions about men making decisions and formulating viewpoints into the neutral languages of natural science. (See Hampshire's brief discussion of this point in the last chapter of his book *The Freedom of the Individual*.) The problem is to accommodate inside moral philosophy, and suggest methods of dealing with the fact that so much of human conduct is moved by mechanical energy of an egocentric kind. In the moral life the enemy is the fat relentless ego. Moral philosophy is properly, and in the past has sometimes been, the discussion of this ego and of the techniques (if any) for its defeat. In this respect moral philosophy has shared some aims with religion. To say this is of course also to deny that moral philosophy should aim at being neutral.

What is a good man like? How can we make ourselves morally better? Can we make ourselves morally better? These are questions the philosopher should try to answer. We realize on reflection that we know little about good men. There are men in history who are traditionally thought of as having been good (Christ, Socrates, certain saints), but if we try to contemplate these men we find that the information about them is scanty and vague, and that, their great moments apart, it is the simplicity and directness of their diction which chiefly colours our conception of them as good. And if we consider contemporary candidates for goodness, if we know of any, we are likely to find them obscure or else on closer inspection full of frailty. Goodness appears to be both rare and hard to picture. It is perhaps most convincingly met with in simple people—inarticulate, unselfish mothers of large families—but these cases are also the least illuminating.

It is significant that the idea of goodness (and of virtue) has been largely superseded in Western moral philosophy by the idea of rightness, supported perhaps by some conception of sincerity. This is to some extent a natural outcome of the disappearance of a permanent background to human activity: a permanent background, whether provided by God, by Reason, by History, or by the self. The agent, thin as a needle, appears in the quick flash of the choosing will. Yet existentialism itself, certainly in its French and Anglo-Saxon varieties, has, with a certain honesty, made evident the paradoxes of its own assumptions. Sartre tells us that when we deliberate the die is already cast, and Oxford philosophy has developed no serious theory of motivation. The agent's freedom, indeed his moral quality, resides in his choices, and yet we are not told what prepares him for the choices. Sartre can admit, with bravado, that we choose out of some sort of pre-existent condition, which he also confusingly calls a choice, and Richard Hare holds that the identification of mental data, such as 'intentions', is philosophically difficult and we had better say that a man is morally the set of his actual choices. That visible motives do not necessitate acts is taken by Sartre as a cue for asserting an irresponsible freedom as an obscure postulate; that motives do not readily yield to 'introspection' is taken by many British philosophers as an excuse for forgetting them and talking about 'reasons' instead. These views seem both unhelpful to the moral pilgrim and also profoundly unrealistic. Moral choice is often a mysterious matter. Kant thought so, and he pictured the mystery in terms of an indiscernible balance between a pure rational agent and an impersonal mechanism, neither of which represented what we normally think of as personality; much existentialist philosophy is in this respect, though often covertly, Kantian. But should not the mystery of choice be conceived of in some other way?

We have learned from Freud to picture 'the mechanism' as something highly individual and personal, which is at the same time very powerful and not easily understood by its owner. The self of psychoanalysis is certainly substantial enough. The existentialist picture of choice, whether it be surrealist or rational, seems unrealistic, over-optimistic, romantic, because it ignores what appears at least to be a sort of continuous background with a life of its own; and it is surely in the tissue of that life that the secrets of good and evil are to be found. Here neither the inspiring ideas of freedom, sincerity and fiats of will, nor the plain wholesome concept of a rational discernment of duty, seem complex enough to do justice to what we really are. What we really are seems much more like an obscure system of energy out of which choices and visible acts of will emerge at intervals in ways which are often unclear and often dependent on the condition of the system in between the moments of choice.

If this is so, one of the main problems of moral philosophy might be formulated thus: are there any techniques for the purification and reorientation of an energy which is naturally selfish, in such a way that when moments of choice arrive we shall be sure of acting rightly? We shall also have to ask whether, if there are such techniques, they should be simply described, in quasi-psychological terms, perhaps in psychological terms, or whether they can be spoken of in a more systematic philosophical way. I have already suggested that a pessimistic view which claims that goodness is the almost impossible countering of a powerful egocentric mechanism already exists in traditional philosophy and in theology. The technique which Plato thought appropriate to this situation I shall discuss later. Much closer and more familiar to us are the techniques of religion, of which the most widely practised is prayer. What becomes of such a technique in a world without God, and can it be transformed to supply at least part of the answer to our central question?

Prayer is properly not petition, but simply an attention to God which is a form of love. With it goes the idea of grace, of a supernatural assistance to human endeavour which overcomes empirical limitations of personality. What is this attention like, and can those who are not religious believers still conceive of profiting by such an activity? Let us pursue the matter by considering what the traditional object of this attention was like and by what means it affected its worshippers. I shall suggest that God was (or is) a *single perfect transcendent non-representable and necessarily real object of attention*; and I shall go on to suggest that moral philosophy should attempt to retain a central concept which has all these characteristics. I shall consider them one by one, although to a large extent they interpenetrate and overlap.

Let us take first the notion of an object of attention. The religious believer, especially if his God is conceived of as a person, is in the fortunate position of being able to focus his thought upon something which is a source of energy. Such focusing, with such results, is natural to human beings. Consider being in love. Consider too the attempt to check being in love, and the need in such a case of another object to attend to. Where strong emotions of sexual love, or of hatred, resentment, or jealousy are concerned, 'pure will' can usually achieve little. It is small use telling oneself 'Stop being in love, stop feeling resentment, be just.' What is needed is a reorientation which will provide an energy of a different kind, from a different source. Notice the metaphors of orientation and of looking. The neo-Kantian existentialist 'will' is a principle of pure movement. But how ill this describes what it is like for us to alter. Deliberately falling out of love is not a jump of the will, it is the acquiring of new objects of attention and thus of new energies as a result of refocusing. The metaphor of orientation may indeed also cover moments when recognizable 'efforts of will' are made, but explicit efforts of will are only a part of the whole situation. That God, attended to, is a powerful source of (often good) energy is a psychological fact. It is also a psychological fact, and one of importance in moral philosophy, that we can all receive moral help by focusing our attention upon things which are valuable: virtuous people, great art, perhaps (I will discuss this later) the idea of goodness itself. Human beings are naturally 'attached' and when an attachment seems painful or bad it is most readily displaced by another attachment, which an attempt at attention can encourage. There is nothing odd or mystical about this, nor about the fact that our ability to act well 'when the time comes' depends partly, perhaps largely, upon the quality of our habitual objects of attention. 'Whatsoever things are true, whatsoever things are honest, whatsoever things are just, whatsoever things are pure, whatsoever things are lovely, whatsoever things of good report; if there be any virtue, and if there be any praise, think on these things.'

The notion that value should be in some sense unitary, or even that there should be a single supreme value concept, may seem, if one surrenders the idea of God, far from obvious. Why should there not be many different kinds of independent moral values? Why should all be one here? The madhouses of the world are filled with people who are convinced that all is one. It might be said that 'all is one' is a dangerous falsehood at any level except the highest; and can that be discerned at all? That a belief in the unity, and also in the hierarchical order, of the moral world has a psychological importance is fairly evident. The notion that 'it all somehow must make sense', or 'there is a best decision here', preserves from despair: the difficulty is how to entertain this consoling notion in a way which is not false. As soon as any idea is a consolation the tendency to falsify it becomes strong: hence the traditional problem of preventing the idea of God from degenerating in the believer's mind. It is true that the intellect naturally seeks unity; and in the sciences, for instance, the assumption of unity consistently rewards the seeker. But how can this dangerous idea be used in morals? It is useless to ask 'ordinary language' for a judgment, since we are dealing with concepts which are not on display in ordinary language or unambiguously tied up to ordinary words. Ordinary language is not a philosopher.

We might, however, set out from an ordinary language situation by reflecting upon the virtues. The concepts of the virtues, and the familiar words which name them, are important since they help to make certain potentially nebulous areas of experience more open to inspection. If we reflect upon the nature of the virtues we are constantly led to consider their relation to each other. The idea of an 'order' of virtues suggests itself, although it might of course be difficult to state this in any systematic form. For instance, if we reflect upon courage and ask why we think it to be a virtue, what kind of courage is the highest, what distinguishes courage from rashness, ferocity, self-assertion, and so on, we are bound, in our explanation, to use the names of other virtues. The best kind of courage (that which would make a man act unselfishly in a concentration camp) is steadfast, calm, temperate, intelligent, loving. . . . This may not in fact be exactly the right description, but it is the right sort of description. Whether there is a single supreme principle in the united world of the virtues, and whether the name of that principle is love, is something which I shall discuss below. All I suggest here is that reflection rightly tends to unify the moral world, and that increasing moral sophistication reveals increasing unity. What is it like to be just? We come to understand this as we come to understand the relationship between justice and the other virtues. Such a reflection requires and generates a rich and diversified vocabulary for naming aspects of goodness. It is a shortcoming of much contemporary moral philosophy that it eschews discussion of the separate virtues, preferring to proceed directly to some sovereign concept such as sincerity, or authenticity, or freedom, thereby imposing, it seems to me, an unexamined and empty idea of unity, and impoverishing our moral language in an important area.

We have spoken of an 'object of attention' and of an unavoidable sense of 'unity'. Let us now go on to consider, thirdly, the much more difficult idea of 'transcendence'. All that has been said so far could be said without benefit of metaphysics. But now it may be asked: are you speaking of a transcendent authority or of a psychological device? It seems to me that the idea of the transcendent, in some form or other, belongs to morality: but it is not easy to interpret. As with so many of these large elusive ideas, it readily takes on forms which are false ones. There is a false transcendence, as there is a false unity, which is generated by modern empiricism: a transcendence which is in effect simply an exclusion, a relegation of the moral to a shadowy existence in terms of emotive language, imperatives, behaviour patterns, attitudes. 'Value' does not belong inside the world of truth functions, the world of science and factual propositions. So it must live somewhere else. It is then attached somehow to the human will, a shadow clinging to a shadow. The result is the sort of dreary moral solipsism which so many so-called books on ethics purvey. An instrument for criticizing the false transcendence, in many of its forms, has been given to us by Marx in the concept of alienation. Is there, however, any true transcendence, or is this idea always a consoling dream projected by human need on to an empty sky?

It is difficult to be exact here. One might start from the assertion that morality, goodness, is a form of realism. The idea of a really good man living in a private dream world seems unacceptable. Of course a good man may be infinitely eccentric, but he must know certain things about his surroundings, most obviously the existence of other people and their claims. The chief enemy of excellence in morality (and also in art) is personal fantasy: the tissue of self-aggrandizing and consoling wishes and dreams which prevents one from seeing what is there outside one. Rilke said of Cézanne that he did not paint 'I like it', he painted 'There it is.' This is not easy, and requires, in art or morals, a discipline. One might say here that art is an excellent analogy of morals, or indeed that it is in this respect a case of morals. We cease to be in order to attend to the existence of something else, a natural object, a person in need. We can see in mediocre art, where perhaps it is even more clearly seen than in mediocre conduct, the intrusion of fantasy, the assertion of self, the dimming of any reflection of the real world.

It may be agreed that the direction of attention should properly be outward, away from self, but it will be said that it is a long step from the idea of realism to the idea of transcendence. I think, however, that these two ideas are related, and one can see their relation particularly in the case of our apprehension of beauty. The link here is the concept of indestructibility or incorruptibility. What is truly beautiful is 'inaccessible' and cannot be possessed or destroyed. The statue is broken, the flower fades, the experience ceases, but something has not suffered from decay and mortality. Almost anything that consoles us is a fake, and it is not easy to prevent this idea from degenerating into a vague Shelleyan mysticism. In the case of the idea of a transcendent personal God the degeneration of the idea seems scarcely avoidable: theologians are busy at their desks at this very moment trying to undo the results of this degeneration. In the case of beauty, whether in art or in nature, the sense of separateness from the temporal process is connected perhaps with concepts of perfection of form and 'authority' which are not easy to transfer into the field of morals. Here I am not sure if this is an analogy or an instance. It is as if we can see beauty itself in a way in which we cannot see goodness itself. (Plato says this at *Phaedrus* 250E.) I can *experience* the transcendence of the beautiful, but (I think) not the transcendence of the good. Beautiful things contain beauty in a way in which good acts do not exactly contain good, because beauty is partly a matter of the senses. So if we speak of good as transcendent we are speaking of something rather more complicated and which cannot be experienced, even when we see the unselfish man in the concentration camp. One might be tempted to use the word 'faith' here if it could be purged of its religious associations. 'What is truly good is incorruptible and indestructible.' 'Goodness is not in this world.' These sound like highly metaphysical statements. Can we give them any clear meaning or are they just things one 'feels inclined to say'?

I think the idea of transcendence here connects with two separate ideas, both of which I will be further concerned with below *perfection* and *certainty*. Are we not certain that there is a 'true direction' towards better conduct, that goodness 'really matters', and does not that certainty about a standard suggest an idea of permanence which cannot be reduced to psychological or any other set of empirical terms? It is true, and this connects with considerations already put forward under the heading of 'attention', that there is a psychological power which derives from the mere idea of a transcendent object, and one might say further from a transcendent object which is to some extent mysterious. But a reductive analysis in, for instance, Freudian terms, or Marxist terms, seems properly to apply here only to a degenerate form of a conception about which one remains certain that a higher and invulnerable form must exist. The idea admittedly remains very difficult. How is one to connect the realism which must involve a clear-eyed contemplation of the misery and evil of the world with a sense of an uncorrupted good without the latter idea becoming the merest consolatory dream? (I think this puts a central problem in moral philosophy.) Also, what is it for someone, who is not a religious believer and not some sort of mystic, to apprehend some separate 'form' of goodness behind the multifarious cases of good behaviour? Should not this idea be reduced to the much more intelligible notion of the interrelation of the virtues, plus a purely subjective sense of the certainty of judgments?

At this point the hope of answering these questions might

lead us on to consider the next, and closely related 'attributes': *perfection* (absolute good) and *necessary existence.* These attributes are indeed so closely connected that from some points of view they are the same. (Ontological proof.) It may seem curious to wonder whether the idea of perfection (as opposed to the idea of merit or improvement) is really an important one, and what sort of role it can play. Well, is it important to measure and compare things and know just how good they are? In any field which interests or concerns us I think we would say yes. A deep understanding of any field of human activity (painting, for instance) involves an increasing revelation of degrees of excellence and often a revelation of there being in fact little that is very good and nothing that is perfect. Increasing understanding of human conduct operates in a similar way. We come to perceive scales, distances, standards, and may incline to see as less than excellent what previously we were prepared to 'let by'. (This need not of course hinder the operation of the virtue of tolerance: tolerance can be, indeed ought to be, clear-sighted.) The idea of perfection works thus within a field of study, producing an increasing sense of direction. To say this is not perhaps to say anything very startling; and a reductionist might argue that an increasingly refined ability to compare need not imply anything beyond itself. The idea of perfection might be, as it were, empty.

Let us consider the case of conduct. What of the command 'Be ye therefore perfect?' Would it not be more sensible to say 'Be ye therefore slightly improved?' Some psychologists warn us that if our standards are too high we shall become neurotic. It seems to me that the idea of love arises necessarily in this context. The idea of perfection moves, and possibly changes, us (as artist, worker, agent) because it inspires love in the part of us that is most worthy. One cannot feel unmixed love for a mediocre moral standard any more than one can for the work of a mediocre artist. The idea of perfection is also a natural producer of order. In its light we come to see that A, which superficially resembles B, is really better than B. And this can occur, indeed must occur, without our having the sovereign idea in any sense 'taped'. In fact it is in its nature that we cannot get it taped. This is the true sense of the 'indefinability' of the good; which was given a vulgar sense by Moore and his followers. It lies always beyond, and it is from this beyond that it exercises its authority. Here again the word seems naturally in place, and it is in the work of artists that we see the operation most clearly. The true artist is obedient to a conception of perfection to which his work is constantly related and re-related in what seems an external manner. One may of course try to 'incarnate' the idea of perfection by saying to oneself 'I want to write like Shakespeare' or 'I want to paint like Piero'. But of course one knows that Shakespeare and Piero, though almost gods, are not gods, and that one has got to do the thing oneself alone and differently, and that beyond the details of craft and criticism there is only the magnetic non-representable idea of the good which remains not 'empty' so much as mysterious. And thus too in the sphere of human conduct.

It will be said perhaps: are these not simply empirical generalizations about the psychology of effort or improvement, or what status do you wish them to have? Is it just a matter of 'this works' or 'it is as if this were so'? Let us consider what, if our subject of discussion were not Good but God, the reply might be. God exists *necessarily*. Everything else which exists exists contingently. What can this mean? I am assuming that there is no plausible 'proof' of the existence of God except some form of the ontological proof, a 'proof' incidentally which must now take on an increased importance in theology as a result of the recent 'demythologizing'. If considered carefully, however, the ontological proof is seen to be not exactly a proof but rather a clear assertion of faith (it is often admitted to be appropriate only for those already convinced), which could only confidently be made on the basis of a certain amount of experience. This assertion could be put in various ways. The desire for God is certain to receive a response. My conception of God contains the certainty of its own reality. God is an object of love which uniquely excludes doubt and relativism. Such obscure statements would of course receive little sympathy from analytical philosophers, who would divide their content between psychological fact and metaphysical nonsense, and who might remark that one might just as well take 'I know that my Redeemer liveth', as asserted by Handel, as a philosophical argument. Whether they are right about 'God' I leave aside: but what about the fate of 'Good'? The difficulties seem similar. What status can we give to the idea of certainty which does seem to attach itself to the idea of good? Or to the notion that we must receive a return when good is sincerely desired? (The concept of grace can be readily secularized.) What is formulated here seems unlike an 'as if' or a 'it works'. Of course one must avoid here, as in the case of God, any heavy material connotation of the misleading word 'exist'. Equally, however, a purely subjective conviction of certainty, which could receive a ready psychological explanation, seems less than enough. Could the problem really be subdivided without residue by a careful linguistic analyst into parts which he would deem innocuous?

A little light may be thrown on the matter if we return now, after the intervening discussion, to the idea of 'realism' which was used earlier in a normative sense: that is, it was assumed that it was better to know what was real than to be in a state of fantasy or illusion. It is true that human beings cannot bear much reality; and a consideration of what the effort to face reality is like, and what are its techniques, may serve both to illuminate the necessity or certainty which seems to attach to 'the Good'; and also to lead on to a reinterpretation of 'will' and 'freedom' in relation to the concept of love. Here again it seems to me that art is the clue. Art presents the most comprehensible examples of the almost irresistible human tendency to seek consolation in fantasy and also of the effort to resist this and the vision of reality which comes with success. Success in fact is rare. Almost all art is a form of fantasy-consolation and few artists achieve the vision of the real. The talent of the artist can be readily, and is naturally, employed to produce a picture whose purpose is the consolation and aggrandizement of its author and the projection of his personal obsessions and wishes. To silence and expel self, to contemplate and delineate nature with a clear eye, is not easy and demands a moral discipline. A great artist is, in respect of his work, a good man, and, in the true sense, a free man. The consumer of art has an analogous task to its producer: to be disciplined enough to see as much reality in the work as the artist has succeeded in putting into it, and not to 'use it as magic'. The appreciation of beauty in art or nature is not only (for all its difficulties) the easiest available spiritual exercise; it is also a completely adequate entry into (and not just analogy of) the good life, since it is the checking of selfishness in the interest of seeing the real. Of course great artists are 'personalities' and have special styles; even Shakespeare occasionally, though very occasionally, reveals a personal obsession. But the greatest art is 'impersonal' because it shows us the world, our world and not another one, with a clarity which startles and delights us simply because we are not used to looking at the real world at all. Of course, too, artists are pattern-makers. The claims of form and the question of 'how much form' to elicit constitutes one of the chief problems of art. But it is when form is used to isolate, to explore, to display something which is true that we are most highly moved and enlightened. Plato says (*Republic*, VII, 532) that the *technai* have the power to lead the best part of the soul to the view of what is most excellent in reality. This well describes the role of great art as an educator and revealer. Consider what we learn from contemplating the characters of Shakespeare or Tolstoy or the paintings of Velasquez or Titian. What is learnt here is something about the real quality of human nature, when it is envisaged, in the artist's just and compassionate vision, with a clarity which does not belong to the self-centred rush of ordinary life.

It is important too that great art teaches us how real things can be looked at and loved without being seized and used, without being appropriated into the greedy organism of the self. This exercise of *detachment* is difficult and valuable whether the thing contemplated is a human being or the root of a tree or the vibration of a colour or a sound. Unsentimental contemplation of nature exhibits the same quality of detachment: selfish concerns vanish, nothing exists except the things which are seen. Beauty is that which attracts this particular sort of unselfish attention. It is obvious here what is the role, for the artist or spectator, of exactness and good vision: unsentimental, detached, unselfish, objective attention. It is also clear that in moral situations a similar exactness is called for. I would suggest that the authority of the Good seems to us something necessary because the realism (ability to perceive reality) required for goodness is a kind of intellectual ability to perceive what is true, which is automatically at the same time a suppression of self. *The necessity of the good is then an aspect of the kind of necessity involved in any technique for exhibiting fact.* In thus treating realism, whether of artist or of agent, as a moral achievement, there is of course a further assumption to be made in the fields of morals: that true vision occasions right conduct. This could be uttered simply as an enlightening tautology: but I think it can in fact be supported by appeals to experience. The more the separateness and differentness of other people is realized, and the fact seen that another man has needs and wishes as demanding as one's own, the harder it becomes to treat a person as a thing. That it is realism which makes great art great remains too as a kind of proof.

If, still led by the clue of art, we ask further questions about the faculty which is supposed to relate us to what is real and thus bring us to what is good, the idea of compassion or love will be naturally suggested. It is not simply that suppression of self is required before accurate vision can be obtained. The great artist sees his objects (and this is true whether they are sad, absurd, repulsive or even evil) in a light of justice and mercy. The direction of attention is, contrary to nature, outward, away from self which reduces all to a false unity, towards the great surprising variety of the world, and the ability so to direct attention is love.

One might at this point pause and consider the picture of human personality, or the soul, which has been emerging. It is in the capacity to love, that is to *see*, that the liberation of the soul from fantasy consists. The freedom which is a proper human goal is the freedom from fantasy, that is the realism of compassion. What I have called fantasy, the proliferation of blinding self-centred aims and images, is itself a powerful system of energy, and most of what is often called 'will' or 'willing' belongs to this system. What counteracts the system is attention to reality inspired by, consisting of, love. In the case of art and nature such attention is immediately rewarded by the enjoyment of beauty. In the case of morality, although there are sometimes rewards, the idea of a reward is out of place. Freedom is not strictly the exercise of the will, but rather the experience of accurate vision which, when this becomes appropriate, occasions action. It is what lies behind and in between actions and prompts them that is important, and it is this area which should be purified. By the time the moment of choice has arrived the quality of attention has probably determined the nature of the act. This fact produces that curious separation between consciously rehearsed motives and action which is sometimes wrongly taken as an experience of freedom. (*Angst.*) Of course this is not to say that good 'efforts of will' are always useless or always fakes. Explicit and immediate 'willing' can play some part, especially as an inhibiting factor. (The daemon of Socrates only told him what not to do.)

In such a picture sincerity and self-knowledge, those popular merits, seem less important. It is an attachment to what lies outside the fantasy mechanism, and not a scrutiny of the mechanism itself, that liberates. Close scrutiny of the mechanism often merely strengthens its power. 'Self-knowledge', in the sense of a minute understanding of one's own machinery, seems to me, except at a fairly simple level, usually a delusion. A sense of such self-knowledge may of course be induced in analysis for therapeutic reasons, but 'the cure' does not prove the alleged knowledge genuine. Self is as hard to see justly as other things, and when clear vision has been achieved, self is a correspondingly smaller and less interesting object. A chief enemy to such clarity of vision, whether in art or morals, is the system to which the technical name of sado-masochism has been given. It is the peculiar subtlety of this system that, while constantly leading attention and energy back into the self, it can produce, almost all the way as it were to the summit, plausible imitations of what is good. Refined sado-masochism can ruin art which is too good to be ruined by the cruder vulgarities of self-indulgence. One's self is interesting, so one's motives are interesting, and the unworthiness of one's motives is interesting. Fascinating too is the alleged relation of master to slave, of the good self to the bad self which, oddly enough, ends in such curious compromises. (Kafka's struggle with the devil which ends up in bed.) The bad self is prepared to suffer but not to obey until the two selves are friends and obedience has become reasonably easy or at least amusing. In reality the good self is very small indeed, and most of what appears good is not. The truly good is not a friendly tyrant to the bad, it is its deadly foe. Even suffering itself can play a demonic role here, and the ideas of guilt and punishment can be the most subtle tool of the ingenious self. The idea of suffering confuses the mind and in certain contexts (the context of 'sincere self-examination' for instance) can masquerade as a purification. It is rarely this, for unless it is very intense indeed it is far too interesting. Plato does not say that philosophy is the study of suffering, he says it is the study of death (*Phaedo* 64A), and these ideas are totally dissimilar. That moral improvement involves suffering is usually true; but the suffering is the by-product of a new orientation and not in any sense an end in itself.

I have spoken of the real which is the proper object of love, and of knowledge which is freedom. The word 'good' which has been moving about in the discussion should now be more explicitly considered. Can good itself be in any sense 'an object of attention'? And how does this problem relate to 'love of the real'? Is there, as it were, a substitute for prayer, that most profound and effective of religious techniques? If the energy and violence of will, exerted on occasions of choice, seems less important than the quality of attention which determines our real attachments, how do we alter and purify that attention and make it more realistic? Is the *via negativa* of the will, its occasional ability to stop a bad move, the only or most considerable conscious power that we can exert? I think there is something analogous to prayer, though it is something difficult to describe, and which the higher subtleties of the self can often falsify; I am not here thinking of any quasi-religious meditative technique, but of something which belongs to the moral life of the ordinary person. The idea of contemplation is hard to understand and maintain in a world increasingly without sacraments and ritual and in which philosophy has (in many respects rightly) destroyed the old substantial conception of the self. A sacrament provides an external visible place for an internal invisible act of the spirit. Perhaps one needs too an analogy of the concept of the sacrament, though this must be treated with great caution. Behaviouristic ethics denies the importance, because it questions the identity, of anything prior to or apart from action which decisively occurs, 'in the mind'. The apprehension of beauty, in art or in nature, often in fact seems to us like a temporally located spiritual experience which is a source of good energy. It is not easy, however, to extend the idea of such an influential experience to occasions of thinking about people or action, since clarity of thought and purity of attention become harder and more ambiguous when the object of attention is something moral.

It is here that it seems to me to be important to retain the idea of Good as a central point of reflection, and here too we may see the significance of its indefinable and non-representable character. *Good, not will is transcendent.* Will is the natural energy of the psyche which is sometimes employable for a worthy purpose. Good is the focus of attention when an intent to be virtuous co-exists (as perhaps it almost always does) with some unclarity of vision. Here, as I have said earlier, beauty appears as the visible and accessible aspect of the Good. The Good itself is not visible. Plato pictured the good man as eventually able to look at the sun. I have never been sure what to make of this part of the myth. While it seems proper to represent the Good as a centre or focus of attention, yet it cannot quite be thought of as a 'visible' one in that it cannot be experienced or represented or defined. We can certainly know more or less where the sun is; it is not so easy to imagine what it would be like to look at it. Perhaps indeed only the good man knows what this is like; or perhaps to look at the sun is to be gloriously dazzled and to see nothing. What does seem to make perfect sense in the Platonic myth is the idea of the Good as the source of light which reveals to us all things as they really are. All just vision, even in the strictest problems of the intellect, and *a fortiori* when suffering or wickedness have to be perceived, is a moral matter. The same virtues, in the end the same virtue (love), are required throughout, and fantasy (self) can prevent us from seeing a blade of grass just as it can prevent us from seeing another person. An increasing awareness of 'goods' and the attempt (usually only partially successful) to attend to them purely, without self, brings with it an increasing awareness of the unity and interdependence of the moral world. One-seeking intelligence is the image of 'faith'. Consider what it is like to increase one's understanding of a great work of art.

I think it is more than a verbal point to say that what should be aimed at is goodness, and not freedom or right action, although right action, and freedom in the sense of humility, are the natural products of attention to the Good. Of course right action is important in itself, with an importance which is not difficult to understand. But it should provide the starting-point of reflection and not its conclusion. Right action, together with the steady extension of the area of strict obligation, is a proper criterion of virtue. Action also tends to confirm, for better or worse, the background of attachment from which it issues. Action is an occasion for grace, or for its opposite. However, the aim of morality cannot be simply action. Without some more positive conception of the soul as a substantial and continually developing mechanism of attachments, the purification and reorientation of which must be the task of morals, 'freedom' is readily corrupted into self-assertion and 'right action' into some sort of *ad hoc* utilitarianism. If a scientifically minded empiricism is not to swallow up the study of ethics completely, philosophers must try to invent a terminology which shows how our natural psychology can be altered by conceptions which lie beyond its range. It seems to me that the Platonic metaphor of the idea of the Good provides a suitable picture here. With this picture must of course be joined a realistic conception of natural psychology (about which almost all philosophers seem to me to have been too optimistic) and also an acceptance of the utter lack of finality in human life. The Good has nothing to do with purpose, indeed it excludes the idea of purpose. 'All is vanity' is the beginning and the end of ethics. The only genuine way to be good is to be good 'for nothing' in the midst of a scene where every 'natural' thing, including one's own mind, is subject to chance, that is, to necessity. That 'for nothing' is indeed the experienced correlate of the invisibility or non-representable blankness of the idea of Good itself.

I have suggested that moral philosophy needs a new and, to my mind, more realistic, less romantic, terminology if it is to rescue thought about human destiny from a scientifically minded empiricism which is not equipped to deal with the real problems. Linguistic philosophy has already begun to join hands with such an empiricism, and most existentialist thinking seems to me either optimistic romancing or else something positively Luciferian. (Possibly Heidegger is Lucifer in person.) However, at this point someone might say, all this is very well, the only difficulty is that none of it is true. Perhaps indeed all is vanity, all is vanity, and there is no respectable intellectual way of protecting people from despair. The world just is hopelessly evil and should you, who speak of realism, not go all the way towards being realistic about this? To speak of Good in this portentous manner is simply to speak of the old concept of God in a thin disguise. But at least 'God' could play a real consoling and encouraging role. It makes sense to speak of loving God, a person, but very little sense to speak of loving Good, a concept. 'Good' even as a fiction is not likely to inspire, or even be comprehensible to, more than a small number of mystically minded people who, being reluctant to surrender 'God', fake up 'Good' in his image, so as to preserve some kind of hope. The picture is not only purely imaginary, it is not even likely to be effective. It is very much better to rely on simple popular utilitarian and existentialist ideas, together with a little empirical psychology, and perhaps some doctored Marxism, to keep the human race going. Day-to-day empirical common sense must have the last word. All specialized ethical vocabularies are false. The old serious metaphysical quest had better now be let go, together with the out-dated concept of God the Father.

I am often more than half persuaded to think in these terms myself. It is frequently difficult in philosophy to tell whether one is saying something reasonably public and objective, or whether one is merely erecting a barrier, special to one's own temperament, against one's own personal fears. (It is always a significant question to ask about any philosopher: what is he afraid of?) Of course one is afraid that the attempt to be good may turn out to be meaningless, or at best something vague and not very important, or turn out to be as Nietzsche described it, or that the greatness of great art may be an ephemeral illusion. Of the 'status' of my arguments I will speak briefly below. That a glance at the scene prompts despair is certainly the case. The difficulty indeed is to look at all. If one does not believe in a personal God there is no 'problem' of evil, but there is the almost insuperable difficulty of looking properly at evil and human suffering. It is very difficult to concentrate attention upon suffering and sin, in others or in oneself, without falsifying the picture in some way while making it bearable. (For instance, by the sado-masochistic devices I mentioned earlier.) Only the very greatest art can manage it, and that is the only public evidence that it can be done at all. Kant's notion of the sublime, though extremely interesting, possibly even more interesting than Kant realized, is a kind of romanticism. The spectacle of huge and appalling things can indeed exhilarate, but usually in a way that is less than excellent. Much existentialist thought relies upon such a 'thinking reed' reaction which is nothing more than a form of romantic self-assertion. It is not this which will lead a man on to unselfish behaviour in the concentration camp. There is, however, something in the serious attempt to look compassionately at human things which automatically suggests that 'there is more than this'. The 'there is more than this', if it is not to be corrupted by some sort of quasi-theological finality, must remain a very tiny spark of insight, something with, as it were, a metaphysical position but no metaphysical form. But it seems to me that the spark is real, and that great art is evidence of its reality. Art indeed, so far from being a playful diversion of the human race, is the place of its most fundamental insight, and the centre to which the more uncertain steps of metaphysics must constantly return.

As for the élite of mystics, I would say no to the term 'élite'. Of course philosophy has its own terminology, but what it attempts to describe need not be, and I think is not in this case, removed from ordinary life. Morality has always been connected with religion and religion with mysticism. The disappearance of the middle term leaves morality in a situation which is certainly more difficult but essentially the same. The background to morals is properly some sort of mysticism, if by this is meant a non-dogmatic essentially un-formulated faith in the reality of the Good, occasionally connected with experience. The virtuous peasant knows, and I believe he will go on knowing, in spite of the removal or modification of the theological apparatus, although what he knows he might be at a loss to say. This view is of course not amenable even to a persuasive philosophical proof and can easily be challenged on all sorts of empirical grounds. However, I do not think that the virtuous peasant will be without resources. Traditional Christian superstition has been compatible with every sort of conduct from bad to good. There will doubtless be new superstitions; and it will remain the case that some people will manage effectively to love their neighbours. I think the 'machinery of salvation' (if it exists) is essentially the same for all. There is no complicated secret doctrine. We are all capable of criticizing, modifying and extending the area of strict obligation which we have inherited. Good is non-representable and indefinable. We are all mortal and equally at the mercy of necessity and chance. These are the true aspects in which all men are brothers.

On the status of the argument there is perhaps little, or else too much, to say. In so far as there is an argument it has already, in a compressed way, occurred. Philosophical argument is almost always inconclusive, and this one is not of the most rigorous kind. This is not a sort of pragmatism or a philosophy of 'as if'. If someone says, 'Do you then believe that the Idea of the Good exists?' I reply, 'No, not as people used to think that God existed.' All one can do is to appeal to certain areas of experience pointing out certain features, and using suitable metaphors and inventing suitable concepts where necessary to make these features visible. No more, and no less, than this is done by the most empirically minded of linguistic philosophers. As there is no philosophical or scientific proof of total determinism the notion is at least allowable that there is a part of the soul which is free from the mechanism of empirical psychology. I would wish to combine the assertion of such a freedom with a strict and largely empirical view of the mechanism itself. Of the very small area of 'freedom', that in us which attends to the real and is attracted by the good, I would wish to give an equally rigorous and perhaps pessimistic account.

I have not spoken of the role of love in its everyday manifestations. If one is going to speak of great art as 'evidence', is not ordinary human love an even more striking evidence of a transcendent principle of good? Plato was prepared to take it as a starting-point. (There are several starting-points.) One cannot but agree that in some sense this is the most important thing of all; and yet human love is normally too profoundly possessive and also too 'mechanical' to be a place of vision. There is a paradox here about the nature of love itself. That the highest love is in some sense impersonal is something which we can indeed see in art, but which I think we cannot see clearly, except in a very piecemeal manner, in the relationships of human beings. Once again the place of art is unique. The image of the Good as a transcendent magnetic centre seems to me the least corruptible and most realistic picture for us to use in our reflections upon the moral life. Here the philosophical 'proof', if there is one, is the same as the moral 'proof'. I would rely especially upon arguments from experience concerned with the realism which we perceive to be connected with goodness, and with the love and detachment which is exhibited in great art.

I have throughout this paper assumed that 'there is no God' and that the influence of religion is waning rapidly. Both these assumptions may be challenged. What seems beyond doubt is that moral philosophy is daunted and confused, and in many quarters discredited and regarded as unnecessary. The vanishing of the philosophical self, together with the confident filling in of the scientific self, has led in ethics to an inflated and yet empty conception of the will, and it is this that I have been chiefly attacking. I am not sure how far my positive suggestions make sense. The search for unity is deeply natural, but like so many things which are deeply natural may be capable of producing nothing but a variety of illusions. What I feel sure of is the inadequacy, indeed the inaccuracy, of utilitarianism, linguistic behaviourism, and current existentialism in any of the forms with which I am familiar. I also feel sure that moral philosophy ought to be defended and kept in existence as a pure activity, or fertile area, analogous in importance to unapplied mathematics or pure 'useless' historical research. Ethical theory has affected society, and has reached as far as to the ordinary man, in the past, and there is no good reason to think that it cannot do so in the future. For both the collective and the individual salvation of the human race, art is doubtless more important than philosophy, and literature most important of all. But there can be no substitute for pure, disciplined, professional speculation: and it is from these two areas, art and ethics, that we must hope to generate concepts worthy, and also able, to guide and check the increasing power of science.

3

THE SOVEREIGNTY OF GOOD
OVER OTHER CONCEPTS

The development of consciousness in human beings is insepar-
ably connected with the use of metaphor. Metaphors are not
merely peripheral decorations or even useful models, they are
fundamental forms of our awareness of our condition: metaphors of space, metaphors of movement, metaphors of vision.
Philosophy in general, and moral philosophy in particular, has in
the past often concerned itself with what it took to be our most
important images, clarifying existing ones and developing
new ones. Philosophical argument which consists of such
image-play, I mean the great metaphysical systems, is usually
inconclusive, and is regarded by many contemporary thinkers as
valueless. The status and merit of this type of argument raises, of
course, many problems. However, it seems to me impossible to
discuss certain kinds of concepts without resort to metaphor,
since the concepts are themselves deeply metaphorical and cannot be analysed into non-metaphorical components without a
loss of substance. Modern behaviouristic philosophy attempts

such an analysis in the case of certain moral concepts, it seems to me without success. One of the motives of the attempt is a wish to 'neutralize' moral philosophy, to produce a philosophical discussion of morality which does not take sides. Metaphors often carry a moral charge, which analysis in simpler and plainer terms is designed to remove. This too seems to me to be misguided. Moral philosophy cannot avoid taking sides, and would-be neutral philosophers merely take sides surreptitiously. Moral philosophy is the examination of the most important of all human activities, and I think that two things are required of it. The examination should be realistic. Human nature, as opposed to the natures of other hypothetical spiritual beings, has certain discoverable attributes, and these should be suitably considered in any discussion of morality. Secondly, since an ethical system cannot but commend an ideal, it should commend a worthy ideal. Ethics should not be merely an analysis of ordinary mediocre conduct, it should be a hypothesis about good conduct and about how this can be achieved. How can we make ourselves better? is a question moral philosophers should attempt to answer. And if I am right the answer will come partly at least in the form of explanatory and persuasive metaphors. The metaphors which I myself favour and the philosopher under whose banner I am fighting I will make clear shortly.

First, however, I wish to mention very briefly two fundamental assumptions of my argument. If either of these is denied what follows will be less convincing. I assume that human beings are naturally selfish and that human life has no external point or $\tau \epsilon \lambda o \varsigma$. That human beings are naturally selfish seems true on the evidence, whenever and wherever we look at them, in spite of a very small number of apparent exceptions. About the quality of this selfishness modern psychology has had something to tell us. The psyche is a historically determined individual relentlessly looking after itself. In some ways it resembles a machine; in order to operate it needs sources of energy, and it is predisposed to certain patterns of activity. The area of its vaunted freedom of choice is not usually very great. One of its main pastimes is daydreaming. It is reluctant to face unpleasant realities. Its consciousness is not normally a transparent glass through which it views the world, but a cloud of more or less fantastic reverie designed to protect the psyche from pain. It constantly seeks consolation, either through imagined inflation of self or through fictions of a theological nature. Even its loving is more often than not an assertion of self. I think we can probably recognize ourselves in this rather depressing description.

That human life has no external point or τέλος is a view as difficult to argue as its opposite, and I shall simply assert it. I can see no evidence to suggest that human life is not something self-contained. There are properly many patterns and purposes within life, but there is no general and as it were externally guaranteed pattern or purpose of the kind for which philosophers and theologians used to search. We are what we seem to be, transient mortal creatures subject to necessity and chance. This is to say that there is, in my view, no God in the traditional sense of that term; and the traditional sense is perhaps the only sense. When Bonhoeffer says that God wants us to live as if there were no God I suspect he is misusing words. Equally the various metaphysical substitutes for God—Reason, Science, History—are false deities. Our destiny can be examined but it cannot be justified or totally explained. We are simply here. And if there is any kind of sense or unity in human life, and the dream of this does not cease to haunt us, it is of some other kind and must be sought within a human experience which has nothing outside it.

The idea of life as self-enclosed and purposeless is of course not simply a product of the despair of our own age. It is the natural product of the advance of science and has developed over a long period. It has already in fact occasioned a whole era in the history of philosophy, beginning with Kant and leading on to the existentialism and the analytic philosophy of the present day. The chief characteristic of this phase of philosophy can be briefly stated: Kant abolished God and made man God in His stead. We are still living in the age of the Kantian man, or Kantian man-god. Kant's conclusive exposure of the so-called proofs of the existence of God, his analysis of the limitations of speculative reason, together with his eloquent portrayal of the dignity of rational man, has had results which might possibly dismay him. How recognizable, how familiar to us, is the man so beautifully portrayed in the *Grundlegung*, who confronted even with Christ turns away to consider the judgment of his own conscience and to hear the voice of his own reason. Stripped of the exiguous metaphysical background which Kant was prepared to allow him, this man is with us still, free, independent, lonely, powerful, rational, responsible, brave, the hero of so many novels and books of moral philosophy. The *raison d'être* of this attractive but misleading creature is not far to seek. He is the offspring of the age of science, confidently rational and yet increasingly aware of his alienation from the material universe which his discoveries reveal; and since he is not a Hegelian (Kant, not Hegel, has provided Western ethics with its dominating image) his alienation is without cure. He is the ideal citizen of the liberal state, a warning held up to tyrants. He has the virtue which the age requires and admires, courage. It is not such a very long step from Kant to Nietzsche, and from Nietzsche to existentialism and the Anglo-Saxon ethical doctrines which in some ways closely resemble it. In fact Kant's man had already received a glorious incarnation nearly a century earlier in the work of Milton: his proper name is Lucifer.

The centre of this type of post-Kantian moral philosophy is the notion of the will as the creator of value. Values which were previously in some sense inscribed in the heavens and guaranteed by God collapse into the human will. There is no transcendent reality. The idea of the good remains indefinable and empty so that human choice may fill it. The sovereign moral concept is freedom, or possibly courage in a sense which identifies it with freedom, will, power. This concept inhabits a quite separate top level of human activity since it is the guarantor of the secondary values created by choice. Act, choice, decision, responsibility, independence are emphasized in this philosophy of puritanical origin and apparent austerity. It must be said in its favour that this image of human nature has been the inspiration of political liberalism. However, as Hume once wisely observed, good political philosophy is not necessarily good moral philosophy.

This impression is indeed an austere one, but there is something still to be added to it. What place, one might ask, is left in this stern picture of solitary all-responsible man for the life of the emotions? In fact the emotions have a rather significant place. They enter through a back door left open by Kant and the whole romantic movement has followed after. Puritanism and romanticism are natural partners and we are still living with their partnership. Kant held a very interesting theory about the relation of the emotions to the reason. He did not officially recognize the emotions as part of the structure of morality. When he speaks of love he tells us to distinguish between practical love which is a matter of rational actions, and pathological love which is a mere matter of feeling. He wants to segregate the messy warm empirical psyche from the clean operations of the reason. However, in a footnote in the *Grundlegung* he allows a subordinate place to a particular emotion, that of *Achtung*, or respect for the moral law. This emotion is a kind of suffering pride which accompanies, though it does not motivate, the recognition of duty. It is an actual experience of freedom (akin to the existentialist *Angst*), the realization that although swayed by passions we are also capable of rational conduct. A close relation of this concept is Kant's handsome conception of the Sublime. We experience the Sublime when we confront the awful contingency of nature or of human fate and return into ourselves with a proud shudder of rational power. How abject we are, and yet our consciousness is of an infinite value. Here it is Belial not Satan who speaks.

> *For who would lose,*
> *Though full of pain, this intellectual being,*
> *Those thoughts that wander through eternity . . .*

The emotions are allowed to return to the scene as a kind of allowable, rather painful, thrill which is a by-product of our status as dignified rational beings.

What appears in Kant as a footnote and a side-issue takes, however, a central place in the development which his philosophy underwent in the romantic movement. I would sum this up by saying that romanticism tended to transform the idea of death into the idea of suffering. To do this is of course an age-old human temptation. Few ideas invented by humanity have more power to console than the idea of purgatory. To buy back evil by suffering in the embrace of good: what could be more satisfying, or as a romantic might say, more thrilling? Indeed the central image of Christianity lends itself just this illegitimate transformation. The *Imitatio Christi* in the later work of Kierke-gaard is a distinguished instance of romantic self-indulgence on this theme, though it may seem unkind to say this of a great and most endearing writer who really did suffer for telling his society some truths. The idea of a rather exciting suffering freedom soon began to enliven the austerity of the puritan half of the Kantian picture, and with this went a taming and beautifying of the idea of death, a cult of pseudo-death and pseudo-transience. Death becomes *Liebestod*, painful and exhilarating, or at worst charming and sweetly tearful. I speak here of course, not of the great romantic artists and thinkers at their best, but of the general beaten track which leads from Kant to the popular philosophies of the present day. When the neo-Kantian Lucifer gets a glimpse of real death and real chance he takes refuge in sublime emotions and veils with an image of tortured freedom that which has been rightly said to be the proper study of philosophers.

When Kant wanted to find something clean and pure outside the mess of the selfish empirical psyche he followed a sound instinct but, in my view, looked in the wrong place. His inquiry led him back again into the self, now pictured as angelic, and inside this angel-self his followers have tended to remain. I want now to return to the beginning and look again at the powerful energy system of the self-defensive psyche in the light of the question, How can we make ourselves better? With such an opponent to deal with one may doubt whether the idea of the proud, naked will directed towards right action is a realistic and sufficient formula. I think that the ordinary man, with the simple religious conceptions which make sense for him, has usually held a more just view of the matter than the voluntaristic philosopher, and a view incidentally which is in better accord with the findings of modern psychology. Religion normally emphasizes states of mind as well as actions, and regards states of mind as the genetic background of action: pureness of heart, meekness of spirit. Religion provides devices for the purification of states of mind. The believer feels that he needs, and can receive, extra help. 'Not I, but Christ.' The real existence of such help is often used as an argument for the truth of religious doctrines. Of course prayer and sacraments may be 'misused' by the believer as mere instruments of consolation. But, whatever one thinks of its theological context, it does seem that prayer can actually induce a better quality of consciousness and provide an energy for good action which would not otherwise be available. Modern psychology here supports the ordinary person's, or ordinary believer's, instinctive sense of the importance of his states of mind and the availability of supplementary energy. Psychology might indeed prompt contemporary behaviouristic philosophers to re-examine their discarded concepts of 'experience' and 'consciousness'. By opening our eyes we do not necessarily see what confronts us. We are anxiety-ridden animals. Our minds are continually active, fabricating an anxious, usually self-preoccupied, often falsifying veil which partially conceals the world. Our states of consciousness differ in quality, our fantasies and reveries are not trivial and unimportant, they are profoundly connected with our energies and our ability to choose and act. And if quality of consciousness matters, then anything which alters consciousness in the direction of unselfishness, objectivity and realism is to be connected with virtue.

Following a hint in Plato (*Phaedrus* 250) I shall start by speaking of what is perhaps the most obvious thing in our surroundings which is an occasion for 'unselfing', and that is what is popularly called beauty. Recent philosophers tend to avoid this term because they prefer to talk of reasons rather than of experiences. But the implication of experience with beauty seems to me to be something of great importance which should not be by-passed in favour of analysis of critical vocabularies. Beauty is the convenient and traditional name of something which art and nature share, and which gives a fairly clear sense to the idea of quality of experience arid change of consciousness. I am looking out of my window in an anxious and resentful state of mind, oblivious of my surroundings, brooding perhaps on some damage done to my prestige. Then suddenly I observe a hovering kestrel. In a moment everything is altered. The brooding self with its hurt vanity has disappeared. There is nothing now but kestrel. And when I return to thinking of the other matter it seems less important. And of course this is something which we may also do deliberately: give attention to nature in order to clear our minds of selfish care. It may seem odd to start the argument against what I have roughly labelled as 'romanticism' by using the case of attention to nature. In fact I do not think that any of the great romantics really believed that we receive but what we give and in our life alone does nature live, although the lesser ones tended to follow Kant's lead and use nature as an occasion for exalted self-feeling. The great romantics, including the one I have just quoted, transcended 'romanticism'. A self-directed enjoyment of nature seems to me to be something forced. More naturally, as well as more properly, we take a self-forgetful pleasure in the sheer alien pointless independent existence of animals, birds, stones and trees. 'Not how the world is, but that it is, is the mystical.'

I take this starting-point, not because I think it is the most important place of moral change, but because I think it is the most accessible one. It is so patently a good thing to take delight in flowers and animals that people who bring home potted plants and watch kestrels might even be surprised at the notion that these things have anything to do with virtue. The surprise is a product of the fact that, as Plato pointed out, beauty is the only spiritual thing which we love by instinct. When we move from beauty in nature to beauty in art we are already in a more difficult region. The experience of art is more easily degraded than the experience of nature. A great deal of art, perhaps most art, actually is self-consoling fantasy, and even great art cannot guarantee the quality of its consumer's consciousness. However, great art exists and is sometimes properly experienced and even a shallow experience of what is great can have its effect. Art, and by 'art' from now on I mean good art, not fantasy art, affords us a pure delight in the independent existence of what is excellent. Both in its genesis and its enjoyment it is a thing totally opposed to selfish obsession. It invigorates our best faculties and, to use Platonic language, inspires love in the highest part of the soul. It is able to do this partly by virtue of something which it shares with nature: a perfection of form which invites unpossessive contemplation and resists absorption into the selfish dream life of the consciousness.

Art however, considered as a sacrament or a source of good

energy, possesses an extra dimension. Art is less accessible than nature but also more edifying since it is actually a human product, and certain arts are actually 'about' human affairs in a direct sense. Art is a human product and virtues as well as talents are required of the artist. The good artist, in relation to his art, is brave, truthful, patient, humble; and even in non-representational art we may receive intuitions of these qualities. One may also suggest, more cautiously, that non-representational art does seem to express more positively something which is to do with virtue. The spiritual role of music has often been acknowledged, though theorists have been chary of analysing it. However that may be, the representational arts, which more evidently hold the mirror up to nature, seem to be concerned with morality in a way which is not simply an effect of our intuition of the artist's discipline.

These arts, especially literature and painting, show us the peculiar sense in which the concept of virtue is tied on to the human condition. They show us the absolute pointlessness of virtue while exhibiting its supreme importance; the enjoyment of art is a training in the love of virtue. The pointlessness of art is not the pointlessness of a game; it is the pointlessness of human life itself, and form in art is properly the simulation of the self-contained aimlessness of the universe. Good art reveals what we are usually too selfish and too timid to recognize, the minute and absolutely random detail of the world, and reveals it together with a sense of unity and form. This form often seems to us mysterious because it resists the easy patterns of the fantasy, whereas there is nothing mysterious about the forms of bad art since they are the recognizable and familiar rat-runs of selfish day-dream. Good art shows us how difficult it is to be objective by showing us how differently the world looks to an objective vision. We are presented with a truthful image of the human condition in a form which can be steadily contemplated; and indeed this is the only context in which many of us are capable of contemplating it at all. Art transcends selfish and obsessive limitations of personality and can enlarge the sensibility of its consumer. It is a kind of goodness by proxy. Most of all it exhibits to us the connection, in human beings, of clear realistic vision with compassion. The realism of a great artist is not a photographic realism, it is essentially both pity and justice.

Herein we find a remarkable redemption of our tendency to conceal death and chance by the invention of forms. Any story which we tell about ourselves consoles us since it imposes pattern upon something which might otherwise seem intolerably chancy and incomplete. However, human life is chancy and incomplete. It is the role of tragedy, and also of comedy, and of painting to show us suffering without a thrill and death without a consolation. Or if there is any consolation it is the austere consolation of a beauty which teaches that nothing in life is of any value except the attempt to be virtuous. Masochism is the artist's greatest and most subtle enemy. It is not easy to portray death, real death, not fake prettified death. Even Tolstoy did not really manage it in Ivan Ilyich, although he did elsewhere. The great deaths of literature are few, but they show us with an exemplary clarity the way in which art invigorates us by a juxtaposition, almost an identification, of pointlessness and value. The death of Patroclus, the death of Cordelia, the death of Petya Rostov. All is vanity. The only thing which is of real importance is the ability to see it all clearly and respond to it justly which is inseparable from virtue. Perhaps one of the greatest achievements of all is to join this sense of absolute mortality not to the tragic but to the comic. Shallow and Silence. Stefan Trofimovich Verhovensky.

Art then is not a diversion or a side-issue, it is the most educational of all human activities and a place in which the nature of morality can be seen. Art gives a clear sense to many ideas which seem more puzzling when we meet with them elsewhere, and it is a clue to what happens elsewhere. An understanding of any art involves a recognition of hierarchy and authority. There are very evident degrees of merit, there are heights and distances; even Shakespeare is not perfect. Good art, unlike bad art, unlike 'happenings', is something pre-eminently outside us and resistant to our consciousness. We surrender ourselves to its authority with a love which is unpossessive and unselfish. Art shows us the only sense in which the permanent and incorruptible is compatible with the transient; and whether representational or not it reveals to us aspects of our world which our ordinary dull dream-consciousness is unable to see. Art pierces the veil and gives sense to the notion of a reality which lies beyond appearance; it exhibits virtue in its true guise in the context of death and chance.

Plato held that beauty could be a starting-point of the good life, but he came to mistrust art and we can see played out in that great spirit the peculiarly distressing struggle between the artist and the saint. Plato allowed to the beauty of the lovely boy an awakening power which he denied to the beauty of nature or of art. He seems to have come to believe that all art is bad art, a mere fiction and consolation which distorts reality. About nature he seems, in the context of the theory of forms, to have been at least once in doubt. Are there forms of mud, hair and dirt? If there are then nature is redeemed into the area of truthful vision. (My previous argument assumes of course, in Platonic terms, that there are.) Another starting-point, or road, which Plato speaks of more often however is the way of the τέχναι, the sciences, crafts, and intellectual disciplines excluding the arts. I think there is a way of the intellect, a sense in which intellectual disciplines are moral disciplines, and this is not too difficult to discern. There are important bridge ideas between morality and other at first sight different human activities, and these ideas are perhaps most clearly seen in the context of the τέχναι. And as when we use the nature of art as a clue, we may be able to learn more about the central area of morality if we examine what are essentially the same concepts more simply on display elsewhere. I mean such concepts as justice, accuracy, truthfulness, realism, humility, courage as the ability to sustain clear vision, love as attachment or even passion without sentiment or self.

The τέχνη which Plato thought was most important was mathematics, because it was most rigorous and abstract. I shall take an example of a τέχνη more congenial to myself: learning a language. If I am learning, for instance, Russian, I am confronted by an authoritative structure which commands my respect. The task is difficult and the goal is distant and perhaps never entirely attainable. My work is a progressive revelation of something which exists independently of me. Attention is rewarded by a knowledge of reality. Love of Russian leads me away from myself towards something alien to me, something which my consciousness cannot take over, swallow up, deny or make unreal. The honesty and humility required of the student—not to pretend to know what one does not know—is the preparation for the honesty and humility of the scholar who does not even feel tempted to suppress the fact which damns his theory. Of course a τέχνη can be misused; a scientist might feel he ought to give up a certain branch of study if he knew that his discoveries would be used wickedly. But apart from special contexts, studying is normally an exercise of virtue as well as of talent, and shows us a fundamental way in which virtue is related to the real world.

I suggested that we could see most clearly in the case of the τέχναι the nature of concepts very central to morality such as justice, truthfulness or humility. We can see too the growth and the inter-connection of these concepts, as when what looks like mere accuracy at one end looks more like justice or courage, or even love at the other. Developing a Sprachgefühl is developing a judicious respectful sensibility to something which is very like another organism. An intellectual discipline can play the same kind of role as that which I have attributed to art, it can stretch the imagination, enlarge the vision and strengthen the judgment. When Plato made mathematics the king τέχνη he was regarding mathematical thought as leading the mind away from the material world and enabling it to perceive a reality of a new kind, very unlike ordinary appearances. And one might regard other disciplines, history, philology, chemistry, as presenting us with a new kind of subject-matter and showing us a new reality behind appearance. These studies are not only an exercise in virtue, they might be thought of as introductory images of the spiritual life. But they are not the spiritual life itself and the mind which has ascended no farther has not achieved the whole of virtue.

I want now to make a closer approach to the central subject of my argument, the Good. Beauty and the τέχναι are, to use Plato's image, the text written in large letters. The concept Good itself is the much harder to discern but essentially similar text written in small letters. In intellectual disciplines and in the enjoyment of art and nature we discover value in our ability to forget self, to be realistic, to perceive justly. We use our imagination not to escape the world but to join it, and this exhilarates us because of the distance between our ordinary dulled consciousness and an apprehension of the real. The value concepts are here patently tied on to the world, they are stretched as it were between the truth-seeking mind and the world, they are not moving about on their own as adjuncts of the personal will. The authority of morals is the authority of truth, that is of reality. We can see the length, the extension, of these concepts as patient attention transforms accuracy without interval into just discernment. Here too we can see it as natural to the particular kind of creatures that we are that love should be inseparable from justice, and clear vision from respect for the real.

That virtue operates in exactly the same kind of way in the central area of morality is less easy to perceive. Human beings are far more complicated and enigmatic and ambiguous than languages or mathematical concepts, and selfishness operates in a much more devious and frenzied manner in our relations with them. Ignorance, muddle, fear, wishful thinking, lack of tests often make us feel that moral choice is something arbitrary, a matter for personal will rather than for attentive study. Our attachments tend to be selfish and strong, and the transformation of our loves from selfishness to unselfishness is sometimes hard even to conceive of. Yet is the situation really so different? Should a retarded child be kept at home or sent to an institution? Should an elderly relation who is a trouble-maker be cared for or asked to go away? Should an unhappy marriage be continued for the sake of the children? Should I leave my family in order to do political work? Should I neglect them in order to practise my art? The love which brings the right answer is an exercise of justice and realism and really *looking*. The difficulty is to keep the attention fixed upon the real situation and to prevent it from returning surreptitiously to the self with consolations of self-pity, resentment, fantasy and despair. The refusal to attend may even induce a fictitious sense of freedom: I may as well toss a coin. Of course virtue is good habit and dutiful action. But the background condition of such habit and such action, in human beings, is a just mode of vision and a good quality of consciousness. It is a *task* to come to see the world as it is. A philosophy which leaves duty without a context and exalts the idea of freedom and power as a separate top level value ignores this task and obscures the relation between virtue and reality. We act rightly 'when the time comes' not out of strength of will but out of the quality of our usual attachments and with the kind of energy and discernment which we have available. And to this the whole activity of our consciousness is relevant.

The central explanatory image which joins together the different aspects of the picture which I have been trying to exhibit is the concept of Good. It is a concept which is not easy to understand partly because it has so many false doubles, jumped-up intermediaries invented by human selfishness to make the difficult task of virtue look easier and more attractive: History, God, Lucifer, Ideas of power, freedom, purpose, reward, even judgment are irrelevant. Mystics of all kinds have usually known this and have attempted by extremities of language to portray the nakedness and aloneness of Good, its absolute for-nothingness. One might say that true morality is a sort of unesoteric mysticism, having its source in an austere and unconsoled love of the Good. When Plato wants to explain Good he uses the image of the sun. The moral pilgrim emerges from the cave and begins to see the real world in the light of the sun, and last of all is able to look at the sun itself. I want now to comment on various aspects of this extremely rich metaphor.

The sun is seen at the end of a long quest which involves a reorientation (the prisoners have to turn round) and an ascent. It is real, it is out there, but very distant. It gives light and energy and enables us to know truth. In its light we see the things of the world in their true relationships. Looking at it itself is supremely difficult and is unlike looking at things in its light. It is a different kind of thing from what it illuminates. Note the metaphor of 'thing' here. Good is a concept about which, and not only in philosophical language, we naturally use a Platonic terminology, when we speak about seeking the Good, or loving the Good. We may also speak seriously of ordinary things, people, works of art, as being good, although we are also well aware of their imperfections. Good lives as it were on both sides of the barrier and we can combine the aspiration to complete goodness with a realistic sense of achievement within our limitations. For all our frailty the command 'be perfect' has sense for us. The concept Good resists collapse into the selfish empirical consciousness. It is not a mere value tag of the choosing will, and functional and casual uses of 'good' (a good knife, a good fellow) are not, as some philosophers have wished to argue, clues to the structure of the concept. The proper and serious use of the term refers us to a perfection which is perhaps never exemplified in the world we know ('There is no good in us') and which carries with it the ideas of hierarchy and transcendence. How do we know that the very great are not the perfect? We see differences, we sense directions, and we know that the Good is still somewhere beyond. The self, the place where we live, is a place of illusion. Goodness is connected with the attempt to see the unself, to see and to respond to the real world in the light of a virtuous consciousness. This is the non-metaphysical meaning of the idea of transcendence to which philosophers have so constantly resorted in their explanations of goodness. 'Good is a transcendent reality' means that virtue is the attempt to pierce the veil of selfish consciousness and join the world as it really is. It is an empirical fact about human nature that this attempt cannot be entirely successful.

Of course we are dealing with a metaphor, but with a very important metaphor and one which is not just a property of philosophy and not just a model. As I said at the beginning, we are creatures who use irreplaceable metaphors in many of our most important activities. And the decent man has probably always, if uncertainly and inexplicably, been able to distinguish between the real Good and its false double. In most ideological contexts virtue can be loved for its own sake. The fundamental metaphors as it were carry this love through and beyond what is false. Metaphors can be a mode of understanding, and so of acting upon, our condition. Philosophers merely do explicitly and systematically and often with art what the ordinary person does by instinct. Plato, who understood this situation better than most of the metaphysical philosophers, referred to many of his theories as 'myths', and tells us that the Republic is to be thought of as an allegory of the soul. 'Perhaps it is a pattern laid up in heaven where he who wishes can see it and become its citizen. But it doesn't matter whether it exists or ever will exist; it is the only city in whose politics [the good man] can take part' (Republic 592).

I want now to continue to explain the concept of the Good and its peculiar relation to other concepts by speaking first of the unifying power of this idea, and secondly of its indefinability. I said earlier that as far as I could see there was no metaphysical unity in human life: all was subject to mortality and chance. And yet we continue to dream of unity. Art is our most ardent dream. In fact morality does actually display to us a sort of unity, though of a peculiar kind and quite unlike the closed theoretical unity of the ideologies. Plato pictures the journeying soul as ascending through four stages of enlightenment, progressively discovering at each stage that what it was treating as realities were only shadows or images of something more real still. At the end of its quest it reaches a non-hypothetical first principle which is the form or idea of the Good, which enables it then to descend and retrace its path, but moving only through the forms or true conception of that which it previously understood only in part (*Republic* 510–11). This passage in the *Republic* has aroused a great deal of discussion but it seems to me that its general application to morality is fairly clear. The mind which has ascended to the vision of the Good can subsequently see the concepts through which it has ascended (art, work, nature, people, ideas, institutions, situations, etc., etc.) in their true nature and in their proper relationships to each other. The good man knows whether and when art or politics is more important than family. The good man sees the way in which the virtues are related to each other. Plato never in fact anywhere expounds a systematic and unitary view of the world of the forms, though he implies that there is a hierarchy of forms. (Truth and Knowledge, for instance, come fairly closely underneath Good, *Republic* 509A). What he does suggest is that we work with the idea of such a hierarchy in so far as we introduce order into our conceptions of the world through our apprehension of Good.

This seems to me to be true. Plato's image implies that complete unity is not seen until one has reached the summit, but moral advance carries with it intuitions of unity which are increasingly less misleading. As we deepen our notions of the virtues we introduce relationship and hierarchy. Courage, which seemed at first to be something on its own, a sort of specialized daring of the spirit, is now seen to be a particular operation of wisdom and love. We come to distinguish a self-assertive ferocity from the kind of courage which would enable a man coolly to choose the labour camp rather than the easy compromise with the tyrant. It would be impossible to have only one virtue unless it were a very trivial one such as thrift. Such transformations as these are cases of seeing the order of the world in the light of the Good and revisiting the true, or more true, conceptions of that which we formerly misconceived. Freedom, we find out, is not an inconsequential chucking of one's weight about, it is the disciplined overcoming of self. Humility is not a peculiar habit of self-effacement, rather like having an inaudible voice, it is selfless respect for reality and one of the most difficult and central of all virtues.

Because of his ambiguous attitude to the sensible world, of which I have already spoken, and because of his confidence in the revolutionary power of mathematics, Plato sometimes seems to imply that the road towards the Good leads away from the world of particularity and detail. However, he speaks of a descending as well as an ascending dialectic and he speaks of a return to the cave. In any case, in so far as goodness is for use in politics and in the market place it must combine its increasing intuitions of unity with an increasing grasp of complexity and detail. False conceptions are often generalized, stereotyped and unconnected. True conceptions combine just modes of judgment and ability to connect with an increased perception of detail. The case of the mother who has to consider each one of her family carefully as she decides whether or not to throw auntie out. This double revelation of both random detail and intuited unity is what we receive in every sphere of life if we seek for what is best. We can see this, once more, quite clearly in art and intellectual work. The great artists reveal the detail of the world. At the same time their greatness is not something peculiar and personal like a proper name. They are great in ways which are to some extent similar, and increased understanding of an art reveals its unity through its excellence. All serious criticism assumes this, though it might be wary of expressing it in a theoretical manner. Art reveals reality and because there is a way in which things are there is a fellowship of artists. Similarly with scholars. Honesty seems much the same virtue in a chemist as in a historian and the evolution of the two could be similar. And there is another similarity between the honesty required to tear up one's theory and the honesty required to perceive the real state of one's marriage, though doubtless the latter is much more difficult. Plato, who is sometimes accused of over-valuing intellectual disciplines, is quite explicit in giving these, when considered on their own, a high but second place. A serious scholar has great merits. But a serious scholar who is also a good man knows not only his subject but the proper place of his subject in the whole of his life. The understanding which leads the scientist to the right decision about giving up a certain study, or leads the artist to the right decision about his family, is superior to the understanding of art and science as such. (Is this not what καίτοι νοητῶν ὄντων μετὰ ἀρχῆς means? Republic 511D.) We are admittedly specialized creatures where morality is concerned and merit in one area does not seem to guarantee merit in another. The good artist is not necessarily wise at home, and the concentration camp guard can be a kindly father. At least this can seem to be so, though I would feel that the artist had at least got a starting-point and that on closer inspection the concentration camp guard might prove to have his limitations as a family man. The scene remains disparate and complex beyond the hopes of any system, yet at the same time the concept Good stretches through the whole of it and gives it the only kind of shadowy unachieved unity which it can possess. The area of morals, and ergo of moral philosophy, can now be seen, not as a hole-and-corner matter of debts and promises, but as covering the whole of our mode of living and the quality of our relations with the world.

Good has often been said to be indefinable for reasons connected with freedom. Good is an empty space into which human choice may move. I want now to suggest that the indefinability of the good should be conceived of rather differently. On the kind of view which I have been offering it seems that we do really know a certain amount about Good and about the way in which it is connected with our condition. The ordinary person does not, unless corrupted by philosophy, believe that he creates values by his choices. He thinks that some things really are better than others and that he is capable of getting it wrong. We are not usually in doubt about the direction in which Good lies. Equally we recognize the real existence of evil: cynicism, cruelty, indifference to suffering. However, the concept of Good still remains obscure and mysterious. We see the world in the light of the Good, but what is the Good itself? The source of vision is not in the ordinary sense seen. Plato says of it 'It is that which every soul pursues and for the sake of which it does all that it does, with some intuition of its nature, and yet also baffled' (Republic 505). And he also says that Good is the source of knowledge and truth and yet is something which surpasses them in splendour (Republic 508–9).

There is a sort of logical, in the modern sense of the word, answer to the question but I think it is not the whole answer. Asking what Good is is not like asking what Truth is or what Courage is, since in explaining the latter the idea of Good must enter in, it is that in the light of which the explanation must proceed. 'True courage is . . .'. And if we try to define Good as X we have to add that we mean of course a good X. If we say that Good is Reason we have to talk about good judgment. If we say that Good is Love we have to explain that there are different kinds of love. Even the concept of Truth has it ambiguities and it is really only of Good that we can say 'it is the trial of itself and needs no other touch'. And with this I agree. It is also argued that all things which are capable of showing degrees of excellence show it in their own way. The idea of perfection can only be exemplified in particular cases in terms of the kind of perfection which is appropriate. So one could not say in general what perfection is, in the way in which one could talk about generosity or good painting. In any case, opinions differ and the truth of judgments of value cannot be demonstrated. This line of argument is sometimes used to support a view of Good as empty and almost trivial, a mere word, 'the most general adjective of commendation', a flag used by the questing will, a term which could with greater clarity be replaced by 'I'm for this.' This argument and its conclusion seem to me to be wrong for reasons which I have already given: excellence has a kind of unity and there are facts about our condition from which lines converge in a definite direction; and also for other reasons which I will now suggest.

A genuine mysteriousness attaches to the idea of goodness and the Good. This is a mystery with several aspects. The indefinability of Good is connected with the unsystematic and inexhaustible variety of the world and the pointlessness of virtue. In this respect there is a special link between the concept of Good and the ideas of Death and Chance. (One might say that Chance is really a subdivision of Death. It is certainly our most effective *memento mori*.) A genuine sense of mortality enables us to see virtue as the only thing of worth; and it is impossible to limit and foresee the ways in which it will be required of us. That we cannot dominate the world may be put in a more positive way. Good is mysterious because of human frailty, because of the immense distance which is involved. If there were angels they might be able to define good but we would not understand the definition. We are largely mechanical creatures, the slaves of relentlessly strong selfish forces the nature of which we scarcely comprehend. At best, as decent persons, we are usually very specialized. We behave well in areas where this can be done fairly easily and let other areas of possible virtue remain undeveloped. There are perhaps in the case of every human being insuperable psychological barriers to goodness. The self is a divided thing and the whole of it cannot be redeemed any more than it can be known. And if we look outside the self what we see are scattered intimations of Good. There are few places where virtue plainly shines: great art, humble people who serve others. And can we, without improving ourselves, really see these things clearly? It is in the context of such limitations that we should picture our freedom. Freedom is, I think, a mixed concept. The true half of it is simply a name of an aspect of virtue concerned especially with the clarification of vision and the domination of selfish impulse. The false and more popular half is a name for the self-assertive movements of deluded selfish will which because of our ignorance we take to be something autonomous.

We cannot then sum up human excellence for these reasons: the world is aimless, chancy, and huge, and we are blinded by self. There is a third consideration which is a relation of the other two. It is difficult to look at the sun: it is not like looking at other things. We somehow retain the idea, and art both expresses and symbolizes it, that the lines really do converge. There is a magnetic centre. But it is easier to look at the converging edges than to look at the centre itself. We do not and probably cannot know, conceptualize, what it is like in the centre. It may be said that since we cannot see anything there why try to look? And is there not a danger of damaging our ability to focus on the sides? I think there is a sense in trying to look, though the occupation is perilous for reasons connected with masochism and other obscure devices of the psyche. The impulse to worship is deep and ambiguous and old. There are false suns, easier to gaze upon and far more comforting than the true one.

Plato has given us the image of this deluded worship in his great allegory. The prisoners in the cave at first face the back wall. Behind them a fire is burning in the light of which they see upon the wall the shadows of puppets which are carried between them and the fire and they take these shadows to be the whole of reality. When they turn round they can see the fire, which they have to pass in order to get out of the cave. The fire, I take it, represents the self, the old unregenerate psyche, that great source of energy and warmth. The prisoners in the second stage of enlightenment have gained the kind of self-awareness which is nowadays a matter of so much interest to us. They can see in themselves the sources of what was formerly blind selfish instinct. They see the flames which threw the shadows which they used to think were real, and they can see the puppets, imitations of things in the real world, whose shadows they used to recognize. They do not yet dream that there is anything else to see. What is more likely than that they should settle down beside the fire, which though its form is flickering and unclear is quite easy to look at and cosy to sit by?

I think Kant was afraid of this when he went to such lengths to draw our attention away from the empirical psyche. This powerful thing is indeed an object of fascination, and those who study its power to cast shadows are studying something which is real. A recognition of its power may be a step towards escape from the cave; but it may equally be taken as an end-point. The fire may be mistaken for the sun, and self-scrutiny taken for goodness. (Of course not everyone who escapes from the cave need have spent much time by the fire. Perhaps the virtuous peasant has got out of the cave without even noticing the fire.) Any religion or ideology can be degraded by the substitution of self, usually in some disguise, for the true object of veneration. However, in spite of what Kant was so much afraid of I think there is a place both inside and outside religion for a sort of contemplation of the Good, not just by dedicated experts but by ordinary people: an attention which is not just the planning of particular good actions but an attempt to look right away from self towards a distant transcendent perfection, a source of uncontaminated energy, a source of new and quite undreamt-of virtue. This attempt, which is a turning of attention away from the particular, may be the thing that helps most when difficulties seem insoluble, and especially when feelings of guilt keep attracting the gaze back towards the self. This is the true mysticism which is morality, a kind of undogmatic prayer which is real and important, though perhaps also difficult and easily corrupted.

I have been speaking of the indefinability of the Good; but is there really nothing else that we can say about it? Even if we cannot find it another name, even if it must be thought of as above and alone, are there not other concepts, or another concept, with which it has some quite special relation? Philosophers have often tried to discern such a relationship: Freedom, Reason, Happiness, Courage, History have recently been tried in the role. I do not find any of these candidates convincing. They seem to represent in each case the philosopher's admiration for some specialized aspect of human conduct which is much less than the whole of excellence and sometimes dubious in itself. I have already mentioned a concept with a certain claim and I will return to that in conclusion. I want now to speak of what is perhaps the most obvious as well as the most ancient and traditional claimant, though one which is rarely mentioned by our contemporary philosophers, and that is Love. Of course Good is sovereign over Love, as it is sovereign over other concepts, because Love can name something bad. But is there not nevertheless something about the conception of a refined love which is practically identical with goodness? Will not 'Act lovingly' translate 'Act perfectly', whereas 'Act rationally' will not? It is tempting to say so.

However I think that Good and Love should not be identified, and not only because human love is usually self-assertive. The concepts, even when the idea of love is purified, still play different roles. We are dealing here with very difficult metaphors. Good is the magnetic centre towards which love naturally moves. False love moves to false good. False love embraces false death. When true good is loved, even impurely or by accident, the quality of the love is automatically refined, and when the soul is turned towards Good the highest part of the soul is enlivened. Love is the tension between the imperfect soul and the magnetic perfection which is conceived of as lying beyond it. (In the *Symposium* Plato pictures Love as being poor and needy.) And when we try perfectly to love what is imperfect our love goes to its object *via* the Good to be thus purified and made unselfish and just. The mother loving the retarded child or loving the tiresome elderly relation. Love is the general name of the quality of attachment and it is capable of infinite degradation and is the source of our greatest errors; but when it is even partially refined it is the energy and passion of the soul in its search for Good, the force that joins us to Good and joins us to the world through Good. Its existence is the unmistakable sign that we are spiritual creatures, attracted by excellence and made for the Good. It is a reflection of the warmth and light of the sun.

Perhaps the finding of other names for Good or the establishing of special relationships cannot be more than a sort of personal game. However I want in conclusion to make just one more move. Goodness is connected with the acceptance of real death and real chance and real transience and only against the background of this acceptance, which is psychologically so difficult, can we understand the full extent of what virtue is like. The acceptance of death is an acceptance of our own nothingness which is an automatic spur to our concern with what is not ourselves. The good man is humble; he is very unlike the big neo-Kantian Lucifer. He is much more like Kierkegaard's tax collector. Humility is a rare virtue and an unfashionable one and one which is often hard to discern. Only rarely does one meet somebody in whom it positively shines, in whom one apprehends with amazement the absence of the anxious avaricious tentacles of the self. In fact any other name for Good must be a partial name; but names of virtues suggest directions of thought, and this direction seems to me a better one than that suggested by more popular concepts such as freedom and courage. The humble man, because he sees himself as nothing, can see other things as they are. He sees the pointlessness of virtue and its unique value and the endless extent of its demand. Simone Weil tells us that the exposure of the soul to God condemns the selfish part of it not to suffering but to death. The humble man perceives the distance between suffering and death. And although he is not by definition the good man perhaps he is the kind of man who is most likely of all to become good.

INDEX

Routledge Classics
Get inside a great mind

Wickedness
A philosophical essay
with a new preface by the author
Mary Midgley

'Mary Midgley is a philosopher with what many have come to admire, and some to fear, as one of the sharpest critical pens in the West.'
Stephen Rose, author of The Conscious Brain

In *Wickedness*, Midgley sets out to delineate not so much the nature of wickedness as its actual sources. Midgley's analysis proves that the capacity for real wickedness is an inevitable part of human nature. She provides us with a framework that accepts the existence of evil yet offers humankind the possibility of rejecting this part of our nature. *Wickedness* offers an understanding of human nature that enhances our very humanity.

Hb: 0–415–25551–1   Pb: 0–415–25398–5

Tractatus Logico-Philosophicus
Ludwig Wittgenstein

'The *Tractatus* is one of the fundamental texts of twentieth-century philosophy – short, bold, cryptic, and remarkable in its power to stir the imagination of philosophers and non-philosophers alike.'
Michael Frayn

Perhaps the most important work of philosophy written in the twentieth century, *Tractatus Logico-Philosophicus* was the only philosophical work that Ludwig Wittgenstein published in his lifetime. He famously summarized the book in the following words: 'What can be said at all can be said clearly; and what we cannot talk about we must pass over in silence.'

Hb: 0–415–25562–7   Pb: 0–415–25408–6

For these and other classic titles from Routledge, visit
www.routledgeclassics.com

Routledge Classics
Get inside a great mind

Writing and Difference
Jacques Derrida

'Almost from the moment deconstruction emerged as a glittering force on the academic scene, its many detractors have been saying that it is "dead". And yet the term deconstruction has penetrated almost every aspect of culture.'
New York Times

In the 1960s a radical concept emerged from the great French thinker Jacques Derrida. He called the new process 'deconstruction'. The academic community was rocked on a scale hitherto unknown, with *Writing and Difference* attracting both accolades and derision. Read the book that changed the way we think; read *Writing and Difference*, the classic introduction.

Hb: 0–415–25537–6   Pb: 0–415–25383–7

Sex and Repression in Savage Society
Bronislaw Malinowski

'No writer of our times has done more than Bronislaw Malinowski to bring together in single comprehension the warm reality of human living and the cool abstractions of science.'
Robert Redfield

In *Sex and Repression in Savage Society* Malinowski, one of the founders of modern anthropology, applied his experiences on the Trobriand Islands to the study of sexuality, and the attendant issues of eroticism, obscenity, incest, oppression, power and parenthood. In so doing, he both utilised and challenged the psychoanalytical methods being popularised at the time in Europe by Freud and others. The result is a unique and brilliant book that, though revolutionary when first published, has since become a standard work on the psychology of sex.

Pb: 0–415–25554–6

For these and other classic titles from Routledge, visit
www.routledgeclassics.com

Routledge Classics
Get inside a great mind

On the Nature of the Psyche
Carl Gustav Jung

'Next to Freud, no psychiatrist of today has advanced our insight into the nature of the psyche more than Jung has.'
Herman Hesse

Jung's discovery of the 'collective unconscious', a psychic inheritance common to all humankind, transformed the understanding of the self and the way we interpret the world. In *On the Nature of the Psyche*, Jung describes this remarkable theory in his own words, and presents a masterly overview of his theories of the unconscious and its relation to the conscious mind. Also contained in this collection is *On Psychic Energy*, where Jung defends his interpretation of the libido, a key factor in the breakdown of his relations with Freud. For anyone seeking to understand Jung's insights into the human mind, this volume is essential reading.

Hb: 0–415–25545–7   Pb: 0–415–25391–8

Modern Man in Search of a Soul
Carl Gustav Jung

'He was more than a psychological or scientific phenomenon; he was to my mind one of the greatest religious phenomena the world has ever experienced.'
Laurens van der Post

Modern Man in Search of a Soul is the perfect introduction to the theories and concepts of one of the most original and influential religious thinkers of the twentieth century. Lively and insightful, it covers all his most significant themes, including man's need for a God and the mechanics of dream analysis. One of his most famous books, it perfectly captures the feelings of confusion that many sense today.

Hb: 0–415–25544–9   Pb: 0–415–25390–X

For these and other classic titles from Routledge, visit

www.routledgeclassics.com

Routledge Classics
Get inside a great mind

The Psychology of Intelligence
Jean Piaget

'He found, to put it most succinctly, that children don't think like grown-ups. . . . Einstein called it a discovery "so simple that only a genius could have thought of it".'
Time

Piaget's theory of learning lies at the very heart of the modern understanding of the human learning process, and he is celebrated as the founding father of child psychology. *The Psychology of Intelligence* is one of his most important works and contains a complete synthesis of his thoughts on the mechanisms of intellectual development. Given his significance, it is hardly surprising that *Psychology Today* pronounced Piaget the best psychologist of the twentieth century.

Pb: 0–415–25401–9

The Language and Thought of the Child
Jean Piaget

'His theory of child development has influenced the way millions of schoolchildren have been taught'
Times Literary Supplement

This classic book is for anyone who has ever wondered how a child develops language, thought and knowledge. Applying for the first time the insights of social psychology and psychoanalysis to the observation of children it has since proved an indispensable source of inspiration and guidance to generations of parents and teachers. While its conclusions remain contentious, few can deny the huge debt we owe to this pioneering work in our continuing attempts to understand the mind of a child.

Pb: 0–415–26750–1

For these and other classic titles from Routledge, visit
www.routledgeclassics.com

Routledge Classics
Get inside a great mind

The Pursuit of Signs
Semiotics, literature, deconstruction with a new preface by the author
Jonathan Culler

'Twenty years ago, if you wanted to know where literary theory was at, I'd say "semiotics", and Culler's *Pursuit of Signs* was the best way to see the links. Today? Same answer. Overview, criticism, problems and solutions: Culler offers them all in each chapter, on key topics and questions of the humanities.'
Mieke Bal, Professor of Theory of Literature, University of Amsterdam

Dancing through semiotics, reader-response criticism, the value of the apostrophe and much more, Jonathan Culler opens up for every reader the closed world of literary criticism. To gain a deeper understanding of the literary movement that has dominated recent Anglo-American literary criticism, *The Pursuit of Signs* is a must.

Hb: 0–415–25536–8   Pb: 0–415–25382–9

Understanding Media
The extensions of man
Marshall McLuhan

'He belongs to that small group of radical dreamers and thinkers who are trying to realize and explore the altered conditions of modern existence . . . When the growth of post-Einsteinian mythologies is recorded, McLuhan's work will have its distinct place. He stands at the frontier.'
George Steiner, Times Literary Supplement

When Marshall McLuhan first coined the phrases 'global village' and 'the medium is the message' in 1964, no one could have predicted today's information-dependant planet. He believed that the message of electronic media foretold the end of humanity as it was known. *Understanding Media* was written twenty years before the PC revolution and thirty years before the rise of the Internet. Yet McLuhan's insights into our engagement with a variety of media led to a complete rethinking of our entire society.

Hb: 0–415–25549–X   Pb: 0–415–25397–7

For these and other classic titles from Routledge, visit

www.routledgeclassics.com

Routledge Classics
Get inside a great mind

Shakespeare's Bawdy
Eric Partridge

'It reads as freshly today as it did fifty years ago, when it surprised everyone with its originality and daring, and intriguing blend of personal insight and solid detective work. If ever a word-book deserved to be called a classic, it is this.'
David Crystal

Regarded by Anthony Burgess as 'a human lexicographer, like Samuel Johnson', Partridge here combines his detailed knowledge of Shakespeare with his unrivalled knowledge of Elizabethan slang and innuendo to open the window upon a long-avoided aspect of Shakespeare's plays. *Shakespeare's Bawdy* is a work of delight and insight that has an appeal that transcends time and class. Acclaimed by Stanley Wells, editor of *The Oxford Shakespeare*, as 'a classic of Shakespeare scholarship', it takes its place alongside other classics with a well-deserved, if slightly cheeky, impunity.

Hb: 0–415–25553–8   Pb: 0–415–25400–0

Romantic Image
with a new epilogue by the author
Frank Kermode

'In this extremely important book of speculative and scholarly criticism Mr Kermode is setting out to redefine the notion of the Romantic tradition, especially in relation to English poetry and criticism ... a rich, packed, suggestive book.'
Times Literary Supplement

One of our most brilliant and accomplished critics, Frank Kermode here redefines our conception of the Romantic movement, questioning both society's harsh perception of the artist as well as poking fun at the artist's occasionally inflated self-image. Written with characteristic wit and style, this ingeniously argued and hugely enjoyable book is a classic of its kind.

Hb: 0–415–26186–4   Pb: 0–415–26817–2

For these and other classic titles from Routledge, visit

www.routledgeclassics.com

Routledge Classics
Get inside a great mind

The Sane Society
Erich Fromm

'Dr Fromm is deeply concerned with the most important unifying questions that can be asked about contemporary western society – is it sane?'
Asa Briggs

Analysing conformity in contemporary patriarchal and capitalistic societies, this searing critique of the status quo was published to wide acclaim and even wider condemnation. A scathing indictment of modern capitalism by one of the twentieth century's greatest political thinkers, this controversial book is arguably more relevant now than at any other time. Read it and decide for yourself – are *you* living in a sane society?

Pb: 0–415–27098–7

The Fear of Freedom
Erich Fromm

'Erich Fromm speaks with wisdom, compassion, learning and insight into the problems of individuals trapped in a social world that is needlessly cruel and hostile.'
Noam Chomsky

Erich Fromm sees right to the heart of our contradictory needs for community and for freedom like no other writer before or since. In *The Fear of Freedom*, Fromm warns that the price of community is indeed high, and it is the individual who pays. He leaves a valuable and original legacy to his readers – a vastly increased understanding of the human character in relation to society.

Hb: 0–415–25542–2   Pb: 0–415–25388–8

For these and other classic titles from Routledge, visit
www.routledgeclassics.com

Routledge Classics
Get inside a great mind

Oppression and Liberty
Simone Weil

'We must simply expose ourselves to the personality of a woman of genius, of a kind of genius akin to that of saints.'
T. S. Eliot

The remarkable French thinker Simone Weil is one of the leading intellectual and spiritual figures of the twentieth century. She explores in *Oppression and Liberty* the political and social implications of individual freedom. Analysing the causes of oppression, its mechanisms and forms, she questions revolutionary responses and presents a prophetic view of a way forward. If 'the future is made of the same stuff as the present', then there will always be a need to continue to listen to Simone Weil.

Hb: 0–415–25560–0   Pb: 0–415–25407–8

The Need for Roots
Simone Weil

'This is one of those books which ought to be studied by the young before their leisure has been lost and their capacity for thought destroyed; books the effect of which, we can only hope, will become apparent in the attitude of mind of another generation.'
T. S. Eliot

Written in the last year of her life, Simone Weil's *The Need for Roots* is a powerful denunciation of the false values of contemporary civilization, setting out a radical vision for spiritual and political renewal to combat a dehumanizing cult of materialism. The book has become an enduring spiritual testament for our age and is the extraordinary final work of one of the most original thinkers of the twentieth century, who possessed, as T. S. Eliot commented, a 'genius akin to saints'.

Hb: 0–415–27101–0   Pb: 0–415–27102–9

For these and other classic titles from Routledge, visit
www.routledgeclassics.com

Routledge Classics
Get inside a great mind

Routledge Classics
Get inside a great mind

Leonardo da Vinci
A Memory of his Childhood
Sigmund Freud

'Freud's *Leonardo* changed the art of biography forever. Henceforth none would be complete without a rummage through the subject's childhood origins.'
Oliver James

The ultimate prodigy, Leonardo da Vinci was an artist of great originality and power, a scientist, and a powerful thinker. According to Sigmund Freud, he was also a flawed, repressed homosexual. The only biography the great psychoanalyst wrote, it remained Freud's favourite composition. The text includes the first full emergence of the concept of narcissism and develops Freud's theories of homosexuality. While based on controversial research, the book offers a fascinating insight into two men – the subject and the author.

Pb: 0–415–25386–1

Michelangelo
with a new preface by Richard Wollheim
Adrian Stokes

Adrian Stokes was one of the twentieth century's finest writers on art and aesthetics and *Michelanglo* is considered to be his most complete work, presenting an understanding of the great artist that no one subsequently uld afford to ignore. Exquisitely written, presenting a rare survey of helangelo's literary as well as his artistic legacy, this book succeeds, as her has before or since, in bringing the artist's greatness nearer into

Pb: 0–415–26765–X

nd other classic titles from Routledge, visit
ww.routledgeclassics.com